THE SOUNDS OF SPOKEN ENGLISH
A MANUAL OF EAR TRAINING FOR ENGLISH STUDENTS

BY

WALTER RIPPMANN

INTRODUCTION

1. That a book dealing with English pronunciation in quite a simple way should yet be intended for English readers rather than for foreigners may seem to require some explanation. "Have I not been talking English all my life?" the reader may ask; "why should I concern myself with the pronunciation of my mother tongue?" If he is quite satisfied with the way in which he speaks, and needs no help in teaching others to speak, then this little book is indeed superfluous—for him; but experience has shown that there are many who are groping about in darkness, anxious for light on the subject. It is above all the teacher who is constantly brought face to face with some difficulty on the part of a pupil. He realises that something is wrong in the pronunciation of a word, but he cannot clearly tell where the fault lies; he trusts that improvement will follow if he repeatedly utters the word correctly pronounced and gets the pupil to say it after him. To his distress the pupil still says the word in the old way, and at last the teacher gives up in despair. When a foreign language is attempted, the difficulties become even more apparent; but these we do not propose to consider here, except in so far as they throw light on our immediate subject, the pronunciation of English.

2. There are several ways of approaching the question. We may turn our attention mainly to the requirements of the public speaker—clergyman, actor, singer, lecturer, reciter, or politician; this is the province of the teachers of elocution. It must be confessed that these have rarely had a scientific training; in many cases they base their teaching on their own experience as reciters and on what their powers of observation have enabled them to learn from their pupils; and they frequently hand on traditions obtained from their own teachers, which may have nothing but old age to recommend them. It is to be feared that the majority of those professing to teach elocution are little better than quacks; and by no one is this more readily acknowledged than by the few who have made an earnest study of the art of public speaking and singing.

The physicist considers the production of sounds from another point of view; he measures the waves of sound with delicate instruments. The physiologist, again, studies the organs of speech in a state of health and sickness.

From all these the phonetician derives assistance. His concern is the spoken language generally. He seeks to ascertain how sounds are produced, and how they are represented in writing; he traces the changes which sounds undergo according to time and place; he attempts to determine the standard of speech for his own time and his own surroundings; he considers how the pronunciation is best imparted to the young and to foreigners.

When the reader has come to the end of this little book, he will see how complicated these problems are, and how much yet awaits solution; he may also have acquired some interest in these problems and desire to give his help. Such help is urgently needed; the number of serious students is distressingly small, and real progress can only be made if their number grows considerably.

3. Reference has been made to the question of **standard speech**; it is convenient to discuss this at once, as the standard selected naturally affects the way in which the subject of English pronunciation is treated.

It is generally agreed that there are two principal types of English speech: Southern English, of which Dr H. Sweet is the best known exponent; and Northern English, which Dr R. J. Lloyd has described in an excellent book. Southern English may be defined as the English spoken in London. The definition will at once strike the reader as requiring some modification—for what form of English is not spoken in London? and the dialect (or rather set of dialects) peculiar to London and known as "cockney" is certainly not to be set up as the standard.

The object of speech is to communicate what is in the mind of the speaker to others; the more adequately it attains this end, the better it is. If there is anything in the manner of speech which attracts attention to itself (for example, "talkin'" in place of "talking," or "'ot" for "hot"), then our attention is distracted from the subject discussed; we say that such faulty speech "jars" upon us. The same is true if the pronunciation is indistinct, or the voice pitched too high, or if the speaker stammers; we then suffer from the strain of listening, and again the object of speech, to communicate thought, is not attained with the least amount of effort. It follows naturally from what has been said that it is our duty towards our fellows to speak in such a way that nothing jars on their ear, nothing strains their attention. To retain certain peculiarities of speech which we know to differ from general usage is nothing short of rudeness. In a great man we may overlook it, in acknowledgment of the services he has rendered to mankind; but we who are in a humbler position must endeavour to render it as easy and pleasant as possible for others to follow what we say.

We are now able to give a better definition of standard speech as considered in this book: it is that form of spoken English which will appear to the majority of educated Londoners as entirely free from unusual features. This speech will be acceptable not only in London, but throughout the south of England; there is reason to believe that it is spreading and nowhere will it be unintelligible or even objectionable.

It must be confessed that on some points there is uncertainty,[1] and these will be discussed later. Language is always changing, and the younger generation does not speak exactly as the older generation does. The standard of to-day will no longer be the standard a hundred years hence. Nevertheless, it is well to inquire what may be regarded as the best speech of our own day, with a view to conforming to this speech and teaching its use to our pupils.

The question may here be raised whether we are to rest content with the standard speech as here defined, or should strive to improve it, for instance by aiming at simple vowels instead of diphthongs, or by carefully uttering consonants which are now commonly dropped. Even if it be desirable, it may well be doubted whether it is possible, so subtle are the changes in our pronunciation, and so unconsciously are they performed. There is a deep-seated tendency to economy of effort, which it would be idle to ignore.

It must always be remembered that the phonetician is primarily concerned with the question how people actually speak; the determination of this must needs precede any attempt to decide how people ought to speak.

In the following pages we shall consider the organs of speech, the various classes of sounds, and how these are produced. Then we inquire into their combination to form words, and the combination of words in sentences.

Incidentally we notice colloquial tendencies, the requirements of public speaking, and other topics arising naturally from our subject.

FOOTNOTES:

[1] It might be thought that reference to a dictionary would be sufficient to settle disputed points. However, it may be said that no dictionary—not even the familiar Webster or the great Oxford English dictionary, now in course of publication—can be implicitly trusted in matters of pronunciation.

THE ORGANS OF SPEECH

4. For speaking we need breath.

In ordinary breathing we take about the same time to draw the breath into the lungs as to let it out. In English speech we use only the breath which is let out; and when we are speaking we accordingly draw it in quickly and let it out slowly. This requires careful adjustment; if we are not careful, our breath gives out in the middle of a sentence. This is one of the things that jar, and must be avoided.

The more breath we can draw in (or inhale) at once, the longer we can use it for speech as we let it out (or exhale it). It is therefore to our advantage to grow accustomed to taking deep breaths, and thus to increase the capacity of the lungs.

"Deep breaths" expresses exactly what is wanted. The lungs are like two elastic bellows. We may expand them only a little; we *can* expand them a great deal. The student should make himself familiar with the shape of the lungs. They occupy the chest, which is a kind of box with elastic sides and bottom. The sides are held out by the ribs, and when the two sets of ribs are drawn apart, the sides of the box are made larger. The bottom of the box (called the diaphragm) is not flat, but rounded, bulging upwards when the lungs are empty. When, however, the diaphragm contracts so that breath is drawn into the lungs to their full capacity, it becomes practically flat. If at the same time we extend the ribs, then we have a considerably increased space for the lungs. Often, however, there is the less satisfactory kind of breathing in which the ribs are not sufficiently active. The descending diaphragm then presses on the soft parts underneath, and this in turn leads to a pushing forward of the abdomen.[2]

Good breathing is essential not only for the singer or the public speaker; it is essential for every teacher and for every pupil. It is necessary for good speech, and it is necessary for good health. The teacher should ascertain as soon as possible whether his pupils are breathing well; a simple test is to determine how long they can hold their breath. They should certainly all be able to do so for forty seconds, and should gradually learn to emit a vowel sound for at least thirty seconds without a pause, and with uniform pitch and volume. Breathing exercises should form a regular part of the pupils' physical training, and the teacher should make a point of drawing the instructor's special attention to pupils whose breathing appears defective.

5. The teacher should also make sure that **the air breathed** is the best procurable under the conditions; he must never relax in his care that the ventilation is good. The results of recent research have not yet been sufficiently taken to heart, and much weariness and ill-health are still due to quite avoidable causes. It may be laid down as an absolute necessity that there should be a pause of at least five minutes in the winter, and at least ten in the summer between consecutive periods of teaching, the periods themselves not exceeding fifty minutes, even in the case of the oldest pupils of school age. During the interval the doors and windows should be thrown wide open, and the room flushed with fresh air. The floor should be either of hard wood treated with "dustless oil" or of cork linoleum. The blackboard should be wiped with a damp cloth, in order to prevent the chalk from vitiating the air. In this way the microbes and particles of dust will be sensibly reduced in number, and the proportion of oxygen in the air will remain satisfactory.

The seats and desks must be of such a kind that the pupils will naturally assume **positions favourable for good breathing.** They must be graduated in size; the seats must have suitably curved backs; and there must be some adjustment by which the edge of the desk will overhang the edge of the seat when the pupils are writing, whereas there is a clear space between them when the pupil stands. This may be obtained either by making the desk as a whole, or the lid of it, move forward and backward; or by making the seat movable. It is not the place here to enter into further details with regard to these important matters; it must suffice to remind the teacher that unceasing perseverance is required. Gently, but firmly, he must insist that his pupils hold themselves well; not stiffly, of course, nor without variety of position. To sit rigidly means a great strain for a child[3]; and it is very desirable that pupils should have frequent opportunities of changing their posture, and especially of resting against the back of the seat.

6. It will often be found that a few minutes given to **breathing exercises** in the middle of a lesson will serve to freshen the pupils. An excellent set of exercises is given in Dr Hulbert's *Breathing for Voice Production* (publ. by Novello), which teachers will do well to read and to put into practice.[4] Many of the throat troubles of which teachers complain are directly due to bad breathing and bad ventilation.

Singing and speaking in chorus, if heartily done by all, may be regarded as admirable breathing exercises, apart from their use in other respects.

A few words with regard to chorus work may be useful to the teacher. If well carried out, it can be of great service. The individual is encouraged to speak up well; it is often found that the class speaking in chorus is better in pronunciation than the majority of those composing it. When a child speaks alone, self-consciousness may make it hesitate or prevent it from raising its voice. But the chorus work must be guided with care and used with moderation. Nothing could surely be more objectionable than the monotonous sing-song into which the reading of a class is almost sure to degenerate if all or nearly all their reading is in chorus. The teacher will guard against this by making the pupils *feel* what they read, and thus insisting on expressive and therefore interesting speech.

Epiglottis.

Left vocal chord.

Right vocal chord.

Cases of mouth-breathing, usually due to adenoid growths, cannot be cured by the teacher; but it is his duty to take the earliest possible notice of such a case, and to ensure that those in charge of the child are warned of the danger incurred by delay in consulting a medical man.

The breath on leaving the lungs passes through the windpipe—and in ordinary breathing there is nothing in its way. In speaking, however, there is often something in its way: a beautiful contrivance, capable of the most varied and delicate adjustment, and known as the **vocal chords.** They are situated where, in a man, we see the "Adam's apple."

The accompanying illustration will serve to explain their nature. It will be seen that the vocal chords spring from both sides of the windpipe. They are really rather of the nature of flexible ridges or shallow flaps than cords. By means of muscles acting on certain cartilages they can be brought closely or lightly together. They consist of a soft fleshy part at one end, and a harder cartilaginous part at the other.

The position of the vocal chords, in other words the nature of the *glottis* (*i.e.* the opening between the vocal chords), modifies the breath in many ways.

When they are apart, in what we may call the rest position, the breath passes through unhindered. When we want a particularly large supply of breath, as in blowing, we keep them still more apart. When we wish to "hold our breath," we close them firmly. When we wish to "clear our throat," we press them together and then let the breath come out in jerks; if this is done violently and (as a rule) unintentionally, a cough is produced; sometimes we do it slightly before the opening vowel of a word spoken emphatically (this is commonly the case in German, and is known as the "glottal stop").

We may also close only the fleshy ends, and leave the cartilaginous ends open; then we speak in a whisper.

7. If we neither leave the vocal chords apart nor bring them together quite closely, but let them touch lightly, then the air as it passes out will make them vibrate; and breath accompanied by this vibration is **voice**[5] in the narrower application of the word. In ordinary speech this vibration is an essential part of all vowels and of many consonants. They are accordingly called **voiced**[6] sounds; those produced without vibration of the vocal chords are **voiceless.**[7]

The vibration can be felt in several ways. Utter a long *s* and then a long *z* (the sounds at the beginning of *seal* and *zeal* respectively), again long *s*, again long *z*, and so on; at the same time put your fingers to your throat, or put your hands to both ears, or lay your hand on the top of your head, and you cannot fail to notice the vibration every time you utter *z*. Try it also with *f v f v f v*, etc., and with the sounds written *s* in *sure* and *z* in *azure*, and the sounds written *th* in *thistle* and *th* in *this*. Then proceed to *p* and *b*, *t* and *d*, *k* and *g* (as in *go*). Lastly, utter a long *ah* with full voice, and then whisper the same sound softly. Ascertain in each case which sound is accompanied by vibration of the vocal chords.

Utter a long *f* and suddenly separate the lower lip from the upper teeth, and nothing more will be heard; but utter a long *v* and again suddenly separate the lip from the teeth, and you will hear the "voice," with a sound like the [ə] described in § 38. (It is the sound uttered when we hesitate in our speech, and is usually represented in writing by "er ... er.")

It is important that the vibration should be good. If it is slow, the pitch will be low; if it is quick, the pitch will be high. But whatever the pitch, the vibration must be uniform. To practise this, dwell on various voiced sounds for a long time, emitting the breath slowly and regularly.

Only the voiced sounds can be produced with varying pitch; they are musical, the rest are noises. Notice, in church for instance, how the tune is carried by the voiced sounds; the voiceless ones seem to break the course of the tune.

When the vocal chords are short they vibrate more quickly than when they are long, and quicker vibrations give a higher pitch. This explains why the average pitch of a woman's voice is higher than that of a man. When a boy's voice "breaks," this is due to certain changes affecting his vocal chords; it is important that the voice should not be subjected to any excessive strain when it is in this stage.

Certain affections of the throat interfere with the action of the vocal chords, and they become incapable of vibrating; then we "lose our voice." When we "lower the voice," we make the vibrations slower, and lower the pitch. When we "drop the voice to a whisper," we are intentionally preventing them from vibrating. This much diminishes the carrying power of the voice, and we thereby ensure that our words are heard only by those who are quite close. A peculiar variety is the "stage aside," when the actor tries to convey the impression that his words are not heard by those near him, yet desires them to be heard by the spectators, many of whom are much farther away. This is a very loud whisper; it naturally requires a considerable effort and is very tiring.

8. The breath which has passed between the vocal chords and issues from the windpipe passes through the mouth, or through the nose, or through both. This is rendered possible by a soft movable flap which can at will be made to close the way through the nose, or—hanging loosely—to leave both passages open. Take a small mirror and look at the inside of your mouth, standing so that as much light as possible falls into it; you will see this flap, the **velum**, hanging down with a kind of V in the centre, the lower extremity of which is known as the *uvula*. Still watching your mouth, inhale through the nose and exhale through the mouth; see how the velum moves as you do this. After a little while try to move the velum, closing and opening the nose passage, without uttering a sound and without breathing.

In French there are four **nasal vowels** (occurring in *un bon vin blanc*) in which the velum hangs loose, and breath passes through nose and mouth. In standard English such vowels do not exist, but another form of nasal vowel, producing a "twang," is sometimes heard in many forms of what may be called dialect speech. The Londoner is often careless about closing the nose passage, and some breath is allowed to pass out by that way so as to be perceptible to the ear in the form of friction, and to impair the quality of the vowels. The "nasal twang" is very noticeable in some forms of American English.

The nasalising tendency may also be observed in untrained singers and public speakers; it is undoubtedly a means of increasing the carrying power of the voice, and of reducing the effort of making oneself understood by a large audience. The same effect can, however, be produced by training the muscles of the chest by means of breathing exercises, and with more agreeable results to the ear.

Pupils who show a tendency to nasalising can be cured by frequent exercises in uttering the mouth (or oral) vowels.

> It is, however, maintained by some teachers of voice production that the best vowel sounds are produced when the velum does not quite prevent the passage of air through the nose.

In producing a **nasal consonant** (such as *m*), we stop the breath somewhere in the mouth (*e.g.* at the lips when we utter *m*), and let it pass out through the nose.

A cold in the nose often prevents the breath from passing through it; and this renders it impossible to produce the nasal consonants *m*, *n*, and *ng* (as in *sing*), the kindred sounds *b*, *d*, and *g* being substituted for them. A similar difficulty is experienced by children with adenoid growths. This is commonly called "speaking through the nose"; it is just the reverse.

9. In speaking, as a rule, the passage to the nose is closed and the breath finds its passage through the mouth. The shape of this passage can be modified in many ways, because several **organs of speech** are movable.

The lower jaw can be moved up and down.

The lips can be closed, or kept lightly touching, or the lower lip may touch the upper teeth; or the lips may be apart, assuming various shapes, from a narrow slit to a large or small circle. They may also be thrust forward, protruded.

The tongue is capable of an even greater variety of position. Again watch the inside of your mouth by means of your little mirror. Say *e* (as in *he*), *a* (as in *father*), *o* (as in *who*), and observe the movements of your tongue; then make the same movements, but without uttering the sounds. You will soon feel how your tongue moves, without needing to look at it. This consciousness of the muscular action of your tongue is valuable, and you must take pains to develop it. Watch the movements of your tongue as you utter other vowel sounds; they will be treated systematically in due course.

By means of these movable organs of speech the mouth passage assumes various forms; it may still be wide enough to leave a free course for the breath, or it may be quite narrow, or it may be closed at some point.

If the passage is free, the result is a **vowel**; if not, it is a **consonant**.[8]

10. If the passage is so narrow at some point that the breath cannot pass through without rubbing or brushing, we have a **continuant** (sometimes called a fricative). Thus when we say *f* or *v*, the breath passes out through the teeth; the only difference between the two sounds being that in saying *v*, the breath is also engaged in setting the vocal chords vibrating. Say *e* (as in *he*) and gradually raise the tongue still further, thus narrowing the passage; you will reach a point when you no longer produce a vowel, but a continuant, namely the sound heard at the beginning of *yes*. These sounds are called continuants, because we can prolong them at will; indeed, we can dwell on them until no more breath is left in the lungs.

11. If the passage is closed altogether at some point, we have a **stop**; the breath is stopped. Say *hope* or *wit* or *luck* and notice how in each case there is a closure at the end. Stops consist of two parts: the closing of the passage, and the subsequent opening of it; this opening resembles a little explosion, and stops are accordingly sometimes called plosives or explosives. Observe that the ear does not require to perceive both the closure and the opening; one is enough to give the impression of the sound. When you say *hope* or *wit* or *luck*, you need only hear the closing of the passage; you can leave your mouth shut, yet to the ear the word will seem complete. (The sound will, however, carry further if you open the passage again; and in public speaking it is therefore to be recommended.) Similarly, in uttering the words *pain, tell, come*, only the opening of the passage is audible; yet the ear is satisfied. In the middle of a word like *night-time*, carefully pronounced, we hear both the closure and the opening; and the interval between the two gives our ear the impression that there are two *t*'s.[9] In quick speech, however, the closure is usually inaudible in such words or, more correctly, the sounds overlap.

12. The narrowing or closing of the passage may be effected at various points. The lips may be partially or completely closed; the lower lip may be pressed against the upper teeth; different parts of the tongue may be pressed against the teeth, or the gums, or the palate. Pass your finger along the roof of your mouth, and notice that only the front of it is hard; we distinguish the hard palate and the soft palate.

13. When we are eating or drinking, the food passes down the gullet, behind the windpipe. To prevent food entering the windpipe, which causes a choking sensation and coughing, there is the *epiglottis* (see the diagram on p. 10), a cartilaginous flap which covers the top of it; this flap is raised when we are breathing. Hence the wisdom of the rule, not to speak while you are eating.

14. In order that speech may have its full effect, it is necessary that the hearer should hear well; this is by no means so common as is generally supposed. The importance of testing the eyesight is now recognised; but the **hearing** is usually neglected. Attention must be drawn to this matter, as teachers often regard pupils as inattentive and dull and reprimand them, when they are really hard of hearing. The teacher's mistake is to some extent pardonable, because the defect is easily overlooked, especially as a pupil may hear badly in one ear and not in the other, and thus seem inattentive only when the teacher happens to be standing on the side of his defective ear. Further, it is a defect which often varies in intensity from day to day, according to the pupil's general condition of health. These considerations point to the urgent necessity of instituting an inspection of the hearing in our schools. The teacher can himself apply the simple test of seeing at what distance the pupil is able to hear whispered double numbers, such as 35, 81; each ear should be tested separately, a cloth being pressed against the other. The teacher will note down the two distances for each pupil, and will probably be surprised at the variations observed. It is clear that defective hearing should constitute a strong claim for a front seat in the class-room, more so than defective eyesight, which can usually be rectified by the use of suitable spectacles.

It is hardly necessary to point out that lack of cleanliness in the ears may interfere with the hearing, and that carelessness with regard to the teeth may lead to their loss and to defects of speech, apart from other unpleasant consequences. It is clear that anything in the nature of tight-lacing renders good breathing impossible; and the fashion of letting the hair cover the ears is also to be discouraged, as rendering the hearing more difficult. In men, tight collars and belts often interfere with the breathing.

15. Lastly, teachers (particularly male teachers) require to be warned against **shouting**; this only tires them and irritates the nerves of their pupils, while the same object can be achieved by careful articulation. Where it is used "to keep the class in order," the teacher should earnestly consider how it is that others can keep order without shouting; usually his difficulties in maintaining discipline are due to ill-health, overstrain, or general incapacity.

When the throat is relaxed, a gargle with some astringent will be found a simple remedy; a solution of alum in water may be recommended for this purpose, or a bit of borax may be held in the cheek.

16. From a very early time the attempt has been made **to represent the spoken language by means of signs.** Picture writing is a primitive and clumsy expedient. It was a great step forward when signs were used to represent syllables, a still further improvement when a separate sign was used for each separate sound.

At first writing was roughly phonetic, in other words, one sign was intended to represent one sound (or set of sounds), and one only; and this is still what is required of an ideal alphabet. It is a commonplace remark that **the English alphabet** largely fails to fulfil this requirement. The same sign represents different sounds (*s*ign, *s*ure, ea*s*y); the same sound is represented by different signs (*c*atch, *k*ill, *q*ueen, la*ck*). Some signs are superfluous (*c*, *x*); sometimes a sound is written, but not pronounced (lam*b*, *k*nee); sometimes two signs, which separately express two sounds, when used together designate a third sound altogether different from these two (*ch* in *ch*at and ri*ch*).

17. How are we to explain this bewildering state of things?

It is due to two causes—the natural development of the language, and the pedantic interference of the learned.

Language is constantly changing. The rate of change is not perhaps always the same, but change there always is. As we have seen above, the older generation and the younger do not speak exactly alike. Now the changes in the spoken language are gradual, and quite unconscious; but a change in the recognised spelling of words is something tangible. It conflicts with a habit we have acquired.

In mediæval times, when there was no printing, no daily paper, no universal compulsory education, there was a good deal of freedom in the spelling, and people wrote very much as they pleased—phonetically, if they were not spoilt by "a little knowledge." But the invention of printing and the dissemination of learning changed all this. A uniform spelling came to be recognised; the nation acquired the habit of regarding it as correct, and would tolerate no deviation from it. Though it represents the pronunciation of a former age, we still use it; and we are quite upset when we read the spellings *labor, center, therefor*, nay even when two words are, contrary to our usage, run together, as in *forever*.

When our spelling received its present form not only was the language very differently pronounced, but the pedantic had already been able to wreak their wicked will on it. Thus the "learned" men of mediæval France spelled *parfaict*, though the *c* of Latin *perfectum* had developed into the *i* of *parfait*, and they did not pronounce the *c* which they introduced into the spelling. The word passed into English, and here also the *c* was at first only written; later on it came to be pronounced. The "learned" similarly introduced a *b* into the French words *douter* and *dette* (because of the Latin *dubitare* and *debita*), but had the good sense to drop it; we have it still in *doubt* and *debt*, though we leave it unpronounced. In later times we find something similar: the learned force us to spell *philosophy* with *ph* and not *f*. The word comes from Greek through Latin; the Greeks pronounced the *ph* actually as *p* plus *h* at the time when the Romans took to spelling Greek words in their language, and these continued to spell *ph* even when the Greeks no longer pronounced *p* plus *h*, but *f*, as we do now.

18. The subject of **spelling reform** is not within the scope of this book; but it presents itself naturally to all who take an intelligent interest in the language. It seems probable that much good will be achieved by the Simplified Spelling Society (44 Great Russell Street, London, W.C.; annual subscription from 1s.), which has been recently established and will undoubtedly profit by the experience of the sister society in the United States. Such spellings as *wel, ful, tho, thoro, bred, plesure*, will surely commend themselves as soon as the eye of the man in the street has been made familiar with them and the etymological sentimentalist has realised the astounding weakness of his arguments.

However distant may be a complete reform, it is certainly helpful to be conscious of the evil; only thus can we neutralize some of its bad effects. The most obvious of these is the lack of **ear training** in our schools, where the mother tongue has been learnt on the basis of the written and not the spoken language. The only method for teaching English reading and writing which can commend itself to the student of the language no less than to the student of childhood is the method identified with the name of Miss Dale. Apart from the sympathy and love of children pervading all her work, it is of unusual importance because she has solved the problem of starting from the spoken language, while avoiding all phonetic symbols.

19. It is, however, convenient for the student of phonetics to have a set of generally accepted signs; otherwise he would be unable to express in writing the pronunciation in such a way that other students could understand what he meant. Without phonetic symbols the designation of sounds becomes awkward. It was one of Miss Dale's many happy thoughts to connect sounds and their written form with definite words, for instance the "moon oo" and the "fern er"; but however suitable that is for the little ones, it is inconvenient for the grown-up student.

There are many phonetic alphabets; all else being equal, the one most widely used is clearly the most valuable. We have therefore chosen for this book **the alphabet of the Association phonétique internationale,** which is already well known in England owing to its use in a number of books for elementary instruction in French, German, and even Latin. It will commend itself to the student by its great simplicity. What will really present difficulty is rather the determination of the actual nature of the spoken word, than the representation of the sounds when once determined.

20. We now give the sounds occurring normally in standard English, and their phonetic signs; the signs for consonants which are likely to be unfamiliar are enclosed.

Consonants.

b   as in *bat*   *rabble*   *tab*
p   as in *pat*   *apple*   *tap*

m	as in *man*	*hammer*	*lamb*
d	as in *dab*	*bidden*	*bad*
t	as in *tap*	*bitten*	*pat*
n	as in *nut*	*winner*	*tun*
g	as in *gut*	*waggle*	*tug*
k	as in *cat*	*tackle*	*tack*
ŋ	as in	*singer*	*sing*
w	as in *wit*		
[10] **ʍ**	as in *when*		
v	as in *van*	*never*	*leave*
f	as in *fan*	*stiffer*	*leaf*
ð	as in *this*	*leather*	*clothe*
θ	as in *thistle*	*Ethel*	*cloth*
z	as in *zeal*	*easel*	*lose*
s	as in *seal*	*lesson*	*lease*
ʒ	as in	*leisure*	*rouge*
ʃ	as in *shed*	*ashes*	*dash*
j	as in *yes*		
r	as in *red*	*very*	
l	as in *lip*	*pallor*	*pill*
h	as in *hot*		

Vowels.

Attention should be paid to the signs for these, as many are unfamiliar. The examples given will convey only a general idea of the sounds, which are discussed in detail in § 36 and foll. The sign : indicates length, and · half length.

i: is the first vowel sound[11] in *bead*.
ɪ is the vowel sound in *bit*.
e: is the first vowel sound[11] in *braid*.
e is the vowel sound in *bet*.
ɛ: is the first vowel sound in *fairy*.
æ is the vowel sound in *bat*.
a is the first vowel sound[11] in *bout, bite*.
ɑ: is the first vowel sound in *father*.
ɔ: is the first vowel sound in *glory*.

ɔ is the vowel sound in *pot*.
o is the first vowel sound[11] in *boat*.
u: is the first vowel sound[11] in *rude*.
ʊ is the vowel sound in *put*.
ə: is the vowel sound in *burn*.
ə is the second vowel sound in *better*.
ʌ is the vowel sound in *but*.

The following sentences written in the conventional and the phonetic spelling will give some idea of the use of this alphabet for representing connected speech as spoken (*a*) very carefully, (*b*) quite colloquially.

For purposes of convenience the ɪ and ʊ are not used in ordinary transcript, as there is no danger of confusion.

(*a*)	The	serious	student	of	phonetics	soon	grows
	ðə	siᵊrjəs	stjuwdənt[12]	əv	foˈnetiks[13]	suwn	grouz
	interested	in	the	subject,	and	every	fresh	speaker
	intərestid	in	ðə	sʌbdʒikt,	ænd	evri	freʃ	spijkə[12]
	presents	new	materials	for	study.
	priˈzents	njuw	məˈtiːᵊriəlz	fə	stʌdi.
(*b*)	Did	you	hear	what	he	told	me	last	night?
	dʒu		hiə	wɔt	i	toul	mi	lɑːs	nait?

FOOTNOTES:

[2] Another defective method of breathing consists in raising the shoulders for the purpose of increasing the capacity of the lungs. The shoulders should, however, not be moved at all in breathing.

[3] The custom of insisting on tightly-folded arms is not to be encouraged.

[4] The exercises suggested by Mr Burrell in *Clear Speaking and Good Reading* (p. 16 and foll.) are also recommended.

[5] Also called tone.

[6] Or, toned.

[7] Or, untoned, breathed.

[8] This definition has its drawbacks, as will be seen later.

[9] Consider what happens in the case of such words as *vintner, lampman*.

[10] It is doubtful whether this can be called a sound of standard English; see § 31.

[11] It is most important that you should not confuse *sound* with *letter*. Thus in bead we have the letters *e* and *a*, which represent vowels in *bed* and *bad*; but the *e* in *bead* has quite a different value from the *e* in *bed*. The two letters *ea* in *bead* together represent two sounds which are described in § 42.

[12] In the *Specimens of English* the diphthongs here represented by [uw] and [ij] are simply printed [u:] and [i:].

[13] Observe that the accent [´] *precedes* the stressed syllable. In the *Specimens of English* the vowel of the stressed syllable is printed in **this type**.

THE SOUNDS CONSIDERED SEPARATELY

Consonants—stops.

21. The sounds which present least difficulty to the student are the stops, in producing which the flow of breath is completely checked. We have already seen in § 11 that every stop, strictly speaking, consists of three parts, the closing and the opening of the passage and the pause between, and that only the closing or only the opening need be heard for the ear to distinguish the sound. The interval between the closure and the opening may be noticeable, in which case we call the consonant double.

Stops may be voiced or voiceless, that is, they may be produced with or without vibration of the vocal chords (see § 7).

Stops may be produced by stopping the breath at some point in the mouth and then letting it burst through the obstacle; these are **oral** stops.

The breath, stopped at some point in the mouth, may be allowed to pass out through the nose; the sounds thus produced are called **nasal**.[14]

Utter the following sounds, and determine whether they are voiced or voiceless, oral or nasal:

[p, g, n, t, b, k, m, d, ŋ.][15]

According to the place of articulation we distinguish lip[16] stops, point[17] stops, front (palate)[18] stops and back (palate)[19] stops.

22. Lip stops.—When the breath is stopped at the lips, three different sounds may be produced.

1. [p], when there has been no vibration of the vocal chords.

In precise or emphatic speech, sufficient breath escapes after the opening of the passage to give the effect of [h][20]; thus *Pay, pay!*[21] [pʰei, pʰei]. This occurs mostly before accented vowels, and sometimes finally[22]: *I hope* [ai houpʰ].[23]

[p] is written *p* or *pp*; rarely *ph* (as in a common pronunciation of *diphtheria* [dipθiːᵊriə], for which see § 27).

Notice the spelling of *hiccough* [hikʌp].

2. [b], when there has been vibration of the vocal chords.

[b] is written *b* or *bb*.

3. [m], when the velum is lowered and part of the breath passes out through the nose. (Generally speaking, this sound is voiced; but when it is immediately followed by a voiceless sound, it may be partly voiced, then voiceless (phonetic sign: m·). Then *lamp* is strictly [læmm·p]. We may say: [m] is **unvoiced** or **devocalized** before a voiceless stop.) Notice the difference in length of [m] in *lamb, hammer, glum, moon*; in which of these words is it short?

In *comfort, triumph* the [m] is often labiodental: the breath is stopped by the upper teeth and lower lip, not by both lips.

In *prism, schism* the *m* may have **syllabic** value; it then does the work usually performed by a vowel. We say [prizəm] or [prizm̩], where [m̩] is the sign for syllabic *m*.

[m] is written *m* or *mm*.

23. In the production of the lip stops the tongue plays no part, except by leaving a free passage; but it is active in the production of the stops we next have to consider. This is therefore the right place to give the names by which we designate the various **parts of the tongue**. We distinguish

the *point*,

the *blade* (above and behind the point when the tongue lies flat),

the *front* (yet further behind), and

the *back*; also

the *ridge* or *dorsum* (an imaginary line drawn along the middle of the top of the tongue from end to end), and

the *rim* (running all round the edge of the tongue when it lies flat).

When the narrowing or closure of the passage is made by the front rim of the tongue, we say it is of *apical* formation; when it is made by the surface of the tongue behind the front rim, we say it is of *dorsal* formation.

24. **Point stops**.[24]—The breath is stopped by the action of the point of the tongue touching the teeth (in which case we have true dentals) or the upper gums (this is known as *alveolar* articulation, "alveoli" being the learned word for the gums). In English the point of the tongue rarely touches the teeth; usually it touches the upper gums, sometimes the hard palate (this should be avoided), in which case it approaches [k]. See the diagram on p. 126.

Hence in careless speech *at last* sometimes becomes [əˈklɑːst].[25] Little children are heard to say [ikl] for *little*; compare also the change from Latin *tremere* to French *craindre*.

Three different sounds may be produced with this stoppage:

1. [t], when there has been no vibration of the vocal chords.

In precise or emphatic speech, sufficient breath escapes after the opening of the passage to give the effect of [h]; thus *take it!* [tʰeik it]. This occurs mostly before accented vowels, and sometimes finally; *he sent me such a charming note* [hi sent mi sʌtʃ ə tʃɑːmiŋ noutʰ].[26]

In certain kinds of uneducated southern English speech [t] is occasionally dropped between vowels, in such words as *water, butter*.

[t] is written *t* or *tt*; *d* in the *ed* of verbs after voiceless sounds, as in *stopped* [stɔpt]; rarely *th*, in words of foreign origin.

2. [d], when there has been vibration of the vocal chords.

[d] is written *d* or *dd*.

3. [n], when the velum is lowered and the breath passes out through the nose. (Generally speaking, this sound is voiced; but when it is immediately preceded or followed by a voiceless sound, it may become voiceless (n̥) in part. Then *sneer* is strictly [sn̥niə], *hint* [hinn̥t].) Notice the difference in length of [n] in *mine, own, manner, an, name*; in which of these words is it long?

In *month, anthem* the [n] is a true dental: the tongue touches the teeth.

In *listen, open* we may have syllabic *n* [n̩]. Compare what was said about syllabic *m* in § 22.

[n] is written *n* or *nn*.

25. Front and back stops.—The breath is stopped by some part of the ridge of the tongue meeting

the front or hard palate, giving *front stops*; or
the back or soft palate, giving *back stops*.

Say [ku] and then [ki]; now whisper them. In which case is the closure more forward in the mouth? Compare with these the place of closure when you say [kɑ].

From these examples it will be seen that the effect for the ear is very much the same, and we shall here make use of the same signs for front and back stops.

In cockney speech there is a distinct tendency to make the closure so far forward that the [k, g] are perceptibly modified. (This pronunciation is suggested by the spelling *gyarden, kyind,* employed by those who try to represent cockney speech.) The "palatalizing" tendency is not to be encouraged; a more effective [k] is produced by distinctly backward articulation. Slight variations in the place of closure due to the place of articulation of neighbouring sounds in a word are inevitable.

Three different sounds may be produced with this stoppage.

1. [k], when there has been no vibration of the vocal chords.

In precise or emphatic speech, sufficient breath escapes after the opening of the passage to give the effect of [h]; thus *come, come!* [kʰʌm, kʰʌm]. This occurs mostly before accented vowels, sometimes finally, *give him a good shake!* [giv im ə gud ʃeikʰ].[27]

[k] is written *c, k, ck, cc* (as in *accuse* [əˊkjuwz]), *ch* (as in *chord* [kɔːd]), *q* (as in *queen* [kwijn]); [ks] as *ks, cc, x, xc*.

2. [g], when there has been vibration of the vocal chords.

Sometimes [g] is pronounced with the tip of the tongue so that it sounds like [d]; thus *glory* becomes *dlory* [dlɔːri]. The way in which [l] is produced (see § 33) explains this.

[g] is written *g* and *gg*; rarely *gh* (as in *ghost* [goust]). For [ks] and [gz] written x see § 30.

3. [ŋ], when the velum is lowered and the breath passes out through the nose. (Generally speaking, this sound is voiced; but when it is immediately followed by a voiceless sound, it may be at first voiced, then voiceless [ŋ̊]; the [ŋ] may be unvoiced (see § 23, 3) before a voiceless stop. Then *length* is strictly [leŋŋ̊θ] or [leŋŋ̊kθ].) Notice the difference in length of [ŋ] in *sing, singer, drink, bang*; in which of these words is it short?

[ŋ] is written *ng*, as in *long* [lɔŋ], and *n* before *g, k*, or *x*, as in *longer* [lɔŋgə], *lank* [læŋk], *lynx* [liŋks]. What does ng represent in *singer*? in *finger*? in *English*?

The "dropping of g" is really an incorrect term. There is no [g] in the ending *-ing* [iŋ];[28] what does take place is the substitution of [n] for [ŋ]. This occurs in baby speech, in vulgar speech, and in the speech of some sections of society. It is on no account to be tolerated.

The opposite mistake is made only by the uneducated, who pronounce *kitchen* as [kitʃiŋ], *chicken* as [tʃikiŋ], and *sudden* as [sʌdiŋ].

Notice the substitution of this sound by the uneducated for the unfamiliar palatal nasal [ɲ] in *Boulogne* [bulɔɲ], the uneducated [bulɔŋ],[29] and for the equally unfamiliar nasal vowel [ɑ̃] in the French word *continent* [kɔ̃tinɑ̃], the uneducated [kɔntinɔŋ].

For [n] becoming [m] or [ŋ] by assimilation, see § 49.

26. Consonants—continuants.

It will be seen that the articulations of these sounds are more difficult to analyse than those of the stops. There is, roughly speaking, only one way of closing a passage entirely; but there are various ways of closing it partially.

The continuants usually go in pairs, one being voiceless, the other voiced.

Lip continuants.—The breath passes between the two lips (hence the term *bilabials*); the tongue is in a position somewhat closer than the [u] position, *i.e.* bunched up at the back (see § 43), and we may therefore call these sounds lip-velar continuants.

The voiced sound [w] is that commonly used in standard English, whether the spelling be *w* or *wh*. In northern English and in Scotch the voiceless [ʍ] is used where the ordinary spelling has *wh*.

It is very doubtful whether [ʍ] has a right to be regarded as a normal sound in standard English. It is taught by professors of elocution, and is therefore commonly heard at recitals and also at amateur theatricals. On the regular stage it is by no means the rule, and in the pulpit it is probably the exception. If it comes naturally to pupils, who bring it with them from the North, they need not be interfered with; there is certainly no good reason why it should be forced on speakers of southern English, who generally produce a grossly exaggerated and quite ludicrous travesty of the northern sound. Which do you use yourself? If [ʍ], is it natural to you, or acquired? Do the rest of your family use it? Any of your friends? What proportion of children in your class?

It may be noted that after voiceless sounds [ʍ] sometimes takes the place of [w], even in standard English; *twenty* is pronounced [twenti] or [tʍenti] and *swim* [swim] or [sʍim]. Sometimes also the sound [ʍ] is heard in *where* pronounced with great emphasis, in the case of speakers who do not ordinarily use it.

It should be noted that these sounds are not continuants in the strict sense of the term, for the lips are gradually brought nearer and gradually drawn apart. The sounds do not *continue* in the same position at all; hence they have been described as "gliding," not "held."

The word *conquer* is sometimes pedantically pronounced [kɔŋkwə] instead of [kɔŋkə]; but it is the rule to sound the [w] in *conquest*. Compare *liquor* [likə], *exchequer* [eks´tʃekə].

A *w* has often influenced a following *a*. Consider the following cases:

was, warm, squabble, quality, quack, quarrel, quaff, wasp, water, waft, walk, swallow.

27. Lip teeth continuants.—The breath passes between the lower lip and the upper teeth (also between the interstices of the upper teeth); the sounds produced in this way are also called *labiodentals*.

The voiceless sound [f] is usually written *f* or *ff*, also *ph* (in words taken from Greek); note also the *gh* in *laugh*, etc.

Notice our reluctance to pronounce *phth* [fθ], as shown in the dropping of *ph* in *phthisis*, and the frequent substitution of *p* for *ph* in *diphtheria, diphthong, naphtha, ophthalmia*, which is, however, avoided by careful speakers.

The voiced sound [v] is usually written *v*.

Sounds very like [f, v] can be produced with both lips. Though they do not ordinarily occur in English, it will be good practice for you to produce them.

When [v] is final, it is not voiced to the end, but passes into whispered [v] (symbol v̭), which sounds very much like voiceless [f]; in other words, the vocal chords cease to vibrate before the breath ceases to pass between the lower lip and the upper teeth. We may say: final [v] is devocalised.

Observe *thief*, but *thieves* and *to thieve*; *loaf*, but *loaves*; *shelf*, but *shelves* and *to shelve*.

The *ph* in *nephew* is pronounced [v], but [f] is heard in dialects.

28. Point continuants.—We have seen above (§ 24) that in English the tongue, as a matter of fact, rarely touches the teeth in the case of point stops. Similarly the narrowing of the passage which leads to the production of point continuants (except [θ,ð]) is not necessarily between the tongue and the teeth; in some cases it is indeed a good deal farther back.

The point continuants include:

1. The hushing, hissing,[30] and lisping sounds, and the *r* sounds, in which the place of articulation is along the middle line of the mouth (*medial* formation); and

2. The *l* sounds, the narrowing for which is between the side rim or rims of the tongue and the side teeth (*lateral* formation).

The *r* sounds and the *l* sounds are sometimes called **liquids**.

29. The hushing sounds.—For the production of the *sh* sounds the passage is narrowed between the blade (see § 23) of the tongue and the hard palate.

A broad current of air is broken against the edge of the teeth. There is some friction between the tongue and the gums, but that against the front teeth is more noticeable.

Watch a Frenchman uttering these sounds, and see what he does with his lips. Do you use your lips in the same way?

The voiceless [ʃ] is usually written *sh*; also *s* after consonants (as in *tension* [tenʃən], *censure* [senʃə]). It is written *ss*, *c* or *t* before a front vowel (*e* or *i*), (as in *passion* [pæʃən], *capricious* [kə´priʃəs], *station* [steiʃən]). In all these cases [ʃ] arose from [sj].

Observe the colloquial pronunciation of *this year* as [ðiʃ jə:]; *six years* [sikʃ jə:z].

The combination [tʃ] is very common, and is usually written *ch* or *tch*. In some cases it arises from [tj], when *t* follows the chief accent of the word and precedes either a front vowel (*e* or *i*) or *u*[31] which goes back to [ju:] (as in *righteous* [raitʃəs], *nature* [neitʃə]). The combination [kʃ] similarly goes back to [ksj] in *anxious* [æŋkʃəs] (notice *anxiety* [æŋ(g)´zaiəti]). *Luxury* is [lʌkʃəri], but *luxurious* is [ləg´zu:riəs] or [ləg´zju:riəs], sometimes [ləg ´ʒu:riəs].

The pronunciation of *associate* as [ə´sousieit],[32] *officiate* as [o´fisieit], instead of [ə´souʃieit, o´fiʃieit], is pedantic; [pro´pisieit] is also faulty for [pro´piʃieit].

The voiced [ʒ] standing alone between vowels is not common in English, being found only where *s* is followed by a front vowel, or by *u* which goes back to [ju:]. Here the development is from [sj] to [zj] and then to [ʒ]. Examples are *vision* [viʒən], *measure* [meʒə]. The spelling *z* is found only in *azure* [æʒə] or [eiʒjə], sometimes [æʒjuə].

Observe the careless pronunciation of *as usual* as [æʒ juwʒuəl], *praise ye the Lord* as [preiʒ jij ðə lɔ:d]. *India rubber* is generally pronounced [indʒə rʌbə].

On the other hand, the combination [dʒ] is quite common. This is written *j* (as in *jet* [dʒet]), *g* before *e* or *i*. (as in *gem* [dʒem], *gin* [dʒin], *age* [eidʒ]; observe also *gaol* [dʒeil]), and sometimes *dg* (as in *edge* [edʒ]). It is spelled *ch* in *ostrich, sandwich, Greenwich, Harwich, Woolwich*, and in *spinach*.

What is the value of *ng* in the following words:—*hang, longing, lounging, language, engage, hunger, hinge, ungraceful*?

30. The hissing sounds.—Distinguish clearly the voiceless [s] as in *seal* and the voiced [z] as in *zeal*. Compare the manner of production of the hissing and the hushing sounds: utter [ʃ] and [s]. (Why will these show the distinction more clearly than [ʒ] and [z]?) You will find that the breath is more widely diffused when you utter [ʃ]; in producing [s] your tongue forms a narrow channel and the breath is thus directed against a point. See the diagram on p. 126.

The usual spelling of both voiceless [s] and voiced [z] is *s*. Notice that

1. The *s* of inflections is [z] after a voiced sound: compare *fills* [filz], *glances* [glɑːnsiz], *dogs* [dɔgz], *faces* [feisiz], but *hits* [hits], *cats* [kæts].

2. The final *s* of some words of one syllable is [z]: *as, has, is, his, was*; but *this, us*.

3. Sometimes the verb has [z], the substantive or adjective [s]:

use [juwz]	*use* [juws]
diffuse [diˊfjuwz]	*diffuse* [diˊfjuws]
close [klouz]	*close* [klous]
lose [luwz]	*loose* [luws]

(Notice the difference in the length of the vowel.)

4. Notice also that we have

[z]	[s]
in *reserve*	in *research*
disease	*disobey*
dissolve	*dissolvent, dissolute*
presumption	*presuppose*

Find other examples (there are many). How do you pronounce *disarm*?

5. *x* represents [ks] in *exercise, excellent,* and in *extra, exceed, express, extol,* but [gz] in *exert, examine, anxiety, exult, exonerate, exorbitant, exotic.*

Do you agree with this statement?

Try to find a rule for the pronunciation of *x*.

In *exile* both pronunciations of *x* may be heard, [ks] being perhaps the more common.

For the dropping of *h* in compounds with *ex-* see § 47.

The voiceless [s] is usually written *s*, but also *ss*, and *c* or *sc* before *e* and *i* (as in *city, scene,* but not in *sceptic* [skeptik]).

Say which of the sounds [ʃ, ʒ, tʃ, dʒ, s, z] occur in the following words:

church, machine, ledger, leisure, seizure, cease, ease, scissors, chisel, lesion, legion, singe, excessive, example.

Notice that final [z] is unvoiced towards the end; thus *is* is strictly [izz̥]; compare what was said about final [v] in § 27.

The term lisping is given to various mispronunciations of the *s* sounds. It may be due to a lasting or a passing malformation of the teeth, palate, or tongue,[33] or it may be simply a bad habit. A slight habitual lisp is often heard, and parents and friends have been known foolishly to encourage a child in the belief that the lisp is "pretty"; it is important to drive this idea out of the child's head. The treatment of lispers is varied; generally they can produce the right sound after some experimenting. When the right sound has been found and distinguished by the child, the rest is entirely a matter of perseverance. There must be frequent repetition in many combinations. The exercises should be practised sparingly at first, and gradually increased, otherwise the strain may be too great and interfere with the child's regular work.

31. The lisping sounds.—Distinguish clearly the voiceless [θ] as in *thistle*, and the voiced [ð] as in *this*. Compare the manner of production of the lisping and the hissing sounds: utter [θ] and [s]. You will find that in the case of [θ] the breath is not passing through a narrow channel, and issues between the tips of the upper teeth and of the tongue. The tongue may be between the teeth, and the sounds are accordingly sometimes called interdental; but this is by no means essential. Our English lisping sounds are usually formed between the point of the tongue and the back of the front upper teeth; part of the tongue fills up the small gap between the teeth, without advancing beyond their back surface.

Which of the following words have [θ] and which have [ð]?

thorn, thou, bath*, baths*, bathe*, then, think, clothe*, cloth*, with, father, thump, lethal, leather, lath, lathe, lithe, loath*, loathe*, breath*, breathe*, heathen, heath, heaths, wreathe*, wreath*, wreaths*, seethe, truth*, truths*.

What do you notice with regard to the words marked with an asterisk? Of what does it remind you in connection with the hissing sounds?

Notice that final [ð] is unvoiced or whispered towards the end; compare what has been said about final [v] and final [z].

A fault, common especially in bad southern English, and found almost invariably in baby speech, is the substitution of [v, f] for [ð, θ]. The baby says [fʌm] for [θʌm], the cockney [nafiŋk] for [nʌθiŋ], [fevə] for [feðə]. This fault should on no account be tolerated; the child (we are of course not referring to the baby) can produce the lisping sounds without difficulty. It need only be told to place the tongue between the teeth. When once the difference in the manner of production of [f] and [θ] is known, the child can also *hear* the difference; all that is now required is perseverance.

In careless speech [h] is sometimes substituted for [θ], thus *I think so* becomes [ai hiŋk sou]. This also has its parallel in baby speech, e.g. [hugə] for *sugar*.

32. The liquids.—This designation comprises the *r* sounds and the *l* sounds.

The sounds written *r* are extremely varied, and are likely to give some trouble to the student. He should in the first place ascertain from his friends (we are assuming that these speak standard English) whether they notice anything peculiar about his *r*. If they do not, it is probable that he uses the untrilled *r*. (The phonetic sign for this is [ɹ], but it is customary to use [r], unless exceptional accuracy be desired.)

This sound is produced by allowing the breath to pass between the raised point of the tongue and the ridge of the upper gums.[34] When the breath makes the tip of the tongue vibrate, we have the trilled or rolled [r]. Can you roll your *r*? Does anyone you know habitually do so? Have you noticed whether Frenchmen or Germans ever do it?

Another kind of *r* is that produced at the back of the mouth, by the help of the uvula (see § 8), and called the throat *r* or uvular *r* (phonetic sign: [R]), as distinguished from the tongue or teeth *r* (lingual or dental *r*). It is not a normal sound in standard English, but is occasionally found. It used to be frequent in Durham and Northumberland (the "Northumbrian burr"), but is dying out there now.

Notice that after [t] and [d] the narrowing for [r] is particularly small, and therefore the friction of the breath particularly noticeable. Say such words as *dry, drink, droll, try, trill, trap,* and carefully observe the nature of the [r]. Notice also that after voiceless sounds the [r] often becomes voiceless [r̥], as in *praise, try, increase.* Sometimes *tried* almost sounds like *chide*, because the passage of the breath is not stopped and the vocal chords have not begun to vibrate. Try to utter a voiceless [r̥] by itself; practise the series [r r̥ r r̥ r].

There is also a peculiar variety of *r* found after *g*, as in *great, green, grass.* This *r* is a kind of palatal blade continuant, and its use should be avoided, as it is generally held to be affected.

In standard English the written *r* is only pronounced initially (as in *red*), between a consonant and a vowel (as in *bread, angry*), and between vowels, the second of which is not only written, but actually pronounced (as in *very*).[35]

It is not pronounced between a vowel and a consonant (as in *arm, lord*), nor when it is final in the spelling or followed by a vowel which is only written and not actually pronounced (as in *bar, bare*). Its place is in many cases taken by the neutral vowel [ə] (see § 38).

Observe that a final *r* is pronounced when the next word begins with a vowel. (Is there anything like this in French?) Thus we say *better* [betə], but [betər ən betə]; *ever* [evə], but [fər evər ənd evə]; *here* [hiə], but [hiᵊr ən ðɛ:ə]; *stir up* [stə:r ʌp], but [stə: ðə faiə]. There is, however, nowadays a tendency to leave even this *r* unpronounced.

The fact that such words as *better* have two forms, with and without [r], has led to the addition of [r] when there is no justification for it. Even educated people are often heard to pronounce *the idea of it* as [ði aidiər əv it]; *The India Office* sometimes becomes [ði indjər ɔfis]; *china ornaments* becomes [tʃainər ɔ:nəmənts]; and clergymen have been known to say [vik´tɔ:jər auə kwijn]. Similarly, in vulgar speech [ðə windər iz oupən], [pə´pɑ:r əz gɔn aut], etc., are quite common.

There is an affected pronunciation of this [ə] which makes it approximate to a deep [ɑ]; the comic papers represent *my dear fellow* as "my deah fellah" to indicate the speech of a swell.

The substitution of [w] for [r] is a mannerism which should not be tolerated; it is the result of a bad habit, not of any defect of the organs of speech.

When a word contains the letter *r* twice, careless speakers incline to drop one of them; *February* becomes [febjuəri], *temporarily* [tempərili], *library* [laibri], *literary* [litəri], *supernumerary* [sjuwpənjuwməri], *contemporary* [kəntempəri]. *Veterinary* usually becomes [vetənri] or [vetnəri].

33. In order to produce the sound of [l], we let the breath pass out between the side rims of the tongue and the side gums and teeth; the point of the tongue touches the roof of the mouth somewhere along the middle line.

Utter [l] with the point of the tongue drawn back as far as possible; then utter [l] several times, gradually bringing the point of the tongue forward, until it eventually touches the teeth. You will notice a difference in the quality of the sound: the sound is "dark"[36] when the tongue is farther back, "clear" when it is forward in the mouth. Notice that when the tongue is drawn back, it is bunched up behind. In standard English the [l] is frequently pronounced with the tongue fairly back in the mouth; the "darkness" of the [l] is particularly noticeable when it comes at the end of a word.[37]

Excessive withdrawal of the tongue tip is not to be encouraged in children; they should rather practise the "clear" [l], though they need not go so far as actually to "let the tongue touch the teeth." This is, however, a good rule, and if instilled in the children will do something to counteract any tendency to "darkness" of the [l]. It is not likely that they will acquire the habit of actually touching the teeth when they say [l]; but a sufficiently "clear" [l] can be obtained if the point of contact is at the upper gums, and even a little farther back than that. It should be noted that the [l] may be "dark," even when the point of the tongue touches the teeth, if the back of the tongue is raised.

In cockney speech the [l] is sometimes lost, through no contact taking place; *tail* is pronounced [tæjɔ] or something similar, with a very open [ɔ] (see § 43) in place of [l], and after consonants also the final *l*, as in *giggle*, is very liable to disappear. This recalls the treatment of final *r* in standard English. In careless speech the [l] also disappears in *only* and in *all right*.

Colonel is pronounced [kə:nəl]; the older spelling *coronel* explains this.

Notice that when [l] comes next to a voiceless sound, it may become partly or wholly voiceless [l̥]. Thus *clear* becomes [kl̥i:ə], *halt* [hɔl̥t]. The friction becomes noticeable then; try to utter [l̥] and observe this. The voiceless sound is the familiar Welsh *ll*.

In *bubble*, *riddle*, etc., we may have syllabic *l* [l]. Compare what was said about syllabic *m* in § 22, and about syllabic *n* in § 24.

The *l* is not pronounced in *calf, half, salve,*[38] *balk, caulk, chalk, falcon,*[39] *folk, stalk, talk, walk, yolk, almond, alms, balm, calm, palm, psalm, qualm, salmon, solder, should, would, could* (where it is not etymologically justified); *golf* is usually [gɔlf], but also [gɔf][3], and rarely [gɔ:f].[40]

It was said above that for [l] we let the breath pass out at both sides of the mouth; but, as a matter of fact, most people let it out only on one side. On which side does it pass out in your own case? Is the same true of your whole family? Ascertain which is the usual side in the case of friends.

34. Front continuants.—Watch with your mirror what the tongue does when you utter the word *he*. You see that it rises in front. Raise it a little more, until the passage becomes quite narrow; the vowel will pass into the sound which we have at the beginning of *yes* [jes], and which we also have in *sue* [sju:w], for which see § 45. As a rule the friction is very slight, and indeed hardly perceptible to the ear; but in the slowly uttered, deliberate *yes* the friction can often be heard very distinctly. The sound is also noteworthy as being, like [w] and [ɹ], "gliding," not "held" (see §§ 26, 32). In careless speech it sometimes passes into [ʒ] after [d]; *during* is pronounced [dʒuwriŋ] instead of [djuwriŋ], the *dew* becomes [dʒuw], *it made you start* [it mei dʒu sta:t]. *Soldier* is regularly pronounced [souldʒə], not [souldjə]; and *verdure, grandeur,* have both pronunciations, [djə] being preferred by careful speakers.

After voiceless sounds, as in *Tuesday, tube,* [j] occasionally passes into the corresponding voiceless [ç], which is the consonant sound in the German *ich*; and sometimes it even becomes [ʃ], compare the careless pronunciation of *don't you know* [dountʃənou], *last year* [la:s tʃiə], *he'll meet you* [hijl mijtʃu]; *I shall hit you* is in vulgar speech [ɑi ʃəl itʃə]. For this development in unstressed syllables, see § 45.

Back continuants.—When we utter the vowel sound of *who* the back of the tongue is raised; if we raise it a little higher, there is friction, and we obtain the back continuants. These do not normally belong to standard English. The voiceless [x] is, however, not uncommon in the pronunciation of words taken from Scotch, Welsh, or German; even in such words [k] is generally substituted. The Scotch *loch* is pronounced [lɔx] or [lɔk]; the German *Hoch(heimer)* is always spelt and pronounced *hock* [hɔk]. In Scotch [x] occurs normally.

Throat r (*uvular* **r**).—This sound, which does not normally belong to standard English, has been referred to in § 32.

35. The h sounds.—We considered the glottis (the interval between the vocal chords) in § 6. We saw that when it is quite open, the breath passes through without producing any audible sound. When, however, the glottis is somewhat narrowed, the breath brushes past the vocal chords, and an *h* is produced; this we may call a voiceless glottal continuant.[41]

Now there may be various kinds of glottal [h]. The passage between the vocal chords may be more or less narrow, and it may remain uniform or gradually grow narrower or wider. The current of breath may be strong or weak; it may be of uniform force, or gradually grow stronger or weaker. When there is a strong current of breath, and the opening is very narrow, we call it "wheezing."

In standard English the *h* is a glottal continuant only when there is precise and emphatic utterance. Ordinarily it is produced in the mouth passage. When we say *ha*, the vocal chords are not drawn together until the vowel is sounded; the mouth, however, gets into position for uttering the vowel a little before the time, and the breath as it passes through produces an *h* sound. In [hɑ] then, we practically have a voiceless [ɑ] followed by the ordinary voiced [ɑ]; in *he*, a voiceless [i] followed by the ordinary [i] vowel; in *who*, a voiceless [u] followed by the ordinary [u]. Whisper these words, and also *hay* and *hoe*; and after each, whisper the [h] only. Notice that the ear detects an actual difference in these *h* sounds.

A good deal depends on the current of breath with which the [h] is uttered. In standard English the current does not keep on growing in volume until the vowel is sounded; it distinctly diminishes before the vowel appears. This may be graphically represented by the signs [<h>].

If the current of breath does not diminish in this way, but starts weakly and does not reach its maximum force until the vowel is reached, the ear does not receive the impression of a distinct [h]. This sound may be written [h<] or simply [<]. This (the "soft breath") precedes initial vowels in standard English; it is the sound which in cockney speech commonly represents the more distinct [<h>]; those who use it are said to "drop their h's." Conscious of the defect, they often prefix a full, even an exaggerated [h] to words which have no *h*. It need hardly be said that carelessness in the use of *h* is not to be tolerated. It is interesting to note that no *h* is ever dropped in the speech of Americans, except in the weak forms of *he, him, her*.

[h] occurs in standard English only before stressed vowels. Initial *h* before unstressed vowels is only pronounced when preceded by a pause.

Notice that:

1. Written *h* is not pronounced in *heir, honest, honour, hour,* and words derived from these.

It is now pronounced in standard English in *herb, hospital, humble, humour* (a fair number of educated speakers still pronounce this word without [h]).

2. It is regarded as correct to say *a history*, but *an historical novel*; *a habit*, but *an habitual action*; many, however, pronounce the *h* in both cases.

3. Certain words drop the *h* when they occur in an unstressed position in the sentence; this is a regular feature of standard colloquial speech, and does not convey the slightest suggestion of vulgarity. It must be recognised that such words have two forms, weak and strong, according as they are used without or with emphasis. Compare the following sentences:

   Tom has been there. Has he though?
   tɔm əz bijn (bin) ðe:ə. hæz i ðou?
   I gave her a book. What, to her?

ai geiv ər ə buk. wɔt, tu hə:?

Find as many words having strong and weak forms as you can by observing the ordinary speech of those around you. Then compare the list given in § 47.

For the dropping of *h* in the second part of compound words, see § 47.

36.

VOWELS

We have considered the sounds produced when the passage through which the breath passes is closed (stops) or narrowed (continuants); we now have to consider the sounds produced when the passage is wide enough for the breath to pass through without audibly brushing against the sides. These sounds are the vowels.

"Voice," produced by the vibration of the vocal chords, may be said to give body to the vowel; the shape of the passage through which the breath passes determines the features that distinguish one vowel from another, *i.e.* its quality. The shape of this passage is capable of almost infinite variation, which leads to a corresponding variety of resonances, and these determine the quality of the vowels.

Picture to yourself the inside of the mouth, and consider how the cavity may become larger or smaller, according as you separate or draw together the jaws; see what a difference it makes if you raise the tongue at the back, or in the middle, or in the front; bear in mind that the position of the lips may also modify the sound, as you will notice if, for instance, you utter [u] as in *who*, first with the lips forming a long narrow slit, and again with the lips forming a very small circle (of the same size as the end of a lead pencil).

37. Of the well-defined vowels that which is articulated with least effort is [ɑ].[42] It is the earliest vowel sound uttered by the baby, before it has acquired control over the muscles of the tongue. It is also common as an interjection. Utter it, and watch the tongue with your mirror; you will see that the middle of the tongue ridge is slightly raised. The opening of the mouth is generally larger than in the case of the other vowels. See the diagram on p. 125.

Utter the standard English sound of *a* in *hat*, for which the sign is [æ]. Say several times [ɑ æ] and watch the tongue as you do so; you will see that it moves forward and is a little higher in front and lower at back for [æ]. The opening of the mouth is often quite as large for [æ] as for [ɑ].

Now try to produce the sound which lies between the two, with the tongue occupying an intermediate position; you will obtain the sound [a], which is the northern English vowel in *hat*, and the vowel in the French word *chat*; in standard English it occurs only as the first part of the diphthongs in *bite* [bait] and *bout* [baut].[43] This [a] is sometimes called the "clear" *a* sound. See the diagram on p. 123.

Next, draw the tongue a little back, and you will obtain a variety of [ɑ] which is "dark" and has a suggestion of the vowel in *all* [ɔ:l]. This sound is commonly substituted for the "pure" or "neutral" [ɑ] in cockney speech, so that *fast* is made to sound like [fɔ:st], *park* like [pɔ:k].

This "darkening" of the *a* sound should not be permitted; in order to counteract it, it may be advisable to make the class utter [ɑ] singly and in chorus, until they are quite clear as to the nature of the required sound.

It is sometimes found that precise speakers, through an excessive desire to avoid any suspicion of cockney leanings in their speech, substitute [a] for [ɑ], saying, for instance, [fa:ðə] in place of [fɑ:ðə]; it is particularly ladies of real or would-be refinement who commit this mistake. A mistake it is, like every other deviation from what is generally recognised by the educated.

In other cases the "clear" pronunciation of *a* is often heard, *e.g.*, in *glass, bath, past, answer, demand, grant, everlasting*. Both [a] and [æ] occur, particularly in the speech of ladies. What is the American pronunciation of *half*?

In standard English there is practically no short [ɑ],[44] but only the long [ɑ:], which should be neither "dark" nor "clear." If we analyse it carefully, we often find[45] that it is not a single vowel of uniform value, only the first part being "pure" [ɑ], the rest being a faint variant; but for practical purposes we may regard it as uniform in quality, as in good speech it is a pure long vowel.

38. There is a short sound closely akin to it (in position, but not in sound), which we have in *but, much,* etc., and for which the sign is [ʌ]. The back of the tongue is raised a little in the production of this sound, and sometimes the front also; and in consequence there are several varieties of it. It occurs only in syllables having some stress; we have [ʌ] in *teacup, unfit, until;* but not in *welcome*, which is not felt to be a compound. When it is unstressed, it becomes the dull vowel [ə]; unstressed *but* is [bət]. Observe the vulgar pronunciation of *just* as [dʒest].

The dull vowel [ə] occurs very commonly in ordinary speech; most unstressed syllables contain this vowel or the variety of [i] mentioned below. It is found, for instance, in the italicised syllables of vow*e*l, vari*e*ty, carp*e*nter, ordin*a*ry. The long [ə:] is variously written; we have it in *fern, fir, fur, word*. (In northern English there is some variety in the [ə], according to the written vowel which it represents.) Notice the precise and the ordinary pronunciation of such words as *paternal, polite, potato*. The uneducated often insert [ə] in such words as *Henry* [henəri], *umbrella* [ʌmbərelə]; and sometimes they substitute [i] for [ə], as in *miracle*, wrongly pronounced [mirikl̩], *philosopher*, wrongly pronounced [fi´lɔsifə], and in *oracle, pigeon*.

The letters *e, i,* and *y* in unstressed syllables represent a very laxly articulated sound, for which the sign [i] is used in this book. It varies somewhat in different speakers; several sounds intermediate between the open [ɪ] and the middle [e] may be heard. This serves to explain the uncertainty of spelling in such cases as *ensure* and *insure, enquire* and *inquire*.

Sometimes the vowel disappears altogether, as in *business, medicine, venison*.

The letter *o* in unstressed syllables preceding the chief stress is usually [ə], but in precise speech an *o*-sound is heard in such words as *conceive, official, possess*. After the chief stress [ɔ] is rarely heard; but *epoch* [ijpɔk] and other uncommon words keep the [ɔ].

39. The front vowels.—Utter the word *he* and notice what the tongue does. You can do so by looking into your mirror, or by putting a finger just inside your front upper teeth, or by whispering the sound, and feeling what happens.

You will generally find that you can analyse vowels best if you whisper them, because the "voice" does not interfere with your appreciation of the mouth resonances. By this time your muscular consciousness (see § 9) should be considerably developed, and you should be conscious of what your tongue, lips, etc., are doing, without having recourse to a mirror.

You will find that you are raising your tongue very high in front: [ɑ] and [i] are extremes; in the one case the front of the tongue is practically as low as it can be, in the other it is raised as high as possible. You might raise the tongue farther, but the resulting sound would not be a vowel. The passage would be too narrow, there would be friction, and a continuant would be the result (see § 34).

Utter a pure [ɑ] and gradually raise the front of the tongue until you reach [i]. You may either keep your vocal chords vibrating all the time, or you may whisper the sounds; but see that the tongue moves slowly and steadily. You will realise that very many sounds lie between [ɑ] and [i]; as they are all produced with the raising of the front of the tongue, they are called front vowels.

We have already noticed clear [a], and have met with [æ], which is the vowel sound in *hat* [hæt]. When unstressed the [æ] gives place to [ə]; *that* [ðæt] becomes [ðət].

The uneducated sometimes substitute a closer sound (the middle *e*) for [æ]; they say [keb] for *cab*, [ketʃ] for *catch*, [θeŋks] for *thanks*, [beŋk] for *bank*. The same mistake may also be heard in the pronunciation of *carriage, radish, January*. In *any, many* the first vowel is always [e]. What is it in *manifold*?

The sound [æ] is only found short. There is a kindred long sound [ɛ:], as in *fair*, for which the tongue is rather higher. It is often called the open [ɛ], [æ] being a still more open sound.

A difference in the formation of [æ] and [ɛː] must be noticed; it is not confined to this pair of vowels. In uttering a vowel sound we may adjust the articulations so favourably that the resulting sound is clear and decided; this may be called *tense* articulation, producing tense vowels. If we do not trouble to adjust the articulations carefully, if we have lax articulation, we obtain *lax* vowels. In standard English we do not articulate tensely, except in precise and emphatic speech. (Notice how tensely the French and the Germans articulate their accented long vowels.) In teaching children the terms *tight* and *loose* may be used.

The articulation of [ɛː] is relatively tense, that of [æ] is lax. For [ɛ] see the diagram on p. 123.

Notice that [ɛː] is always followed by a more or less distinct [ə]; *there* is [ðɛːə], *Mary* is [mɛː(ə)ri]. Consider the value of *-ear-* in *bear* and *bearing*.

There is a vulgar pronunciation of *I dare say* as [ai desei], instead of [ai dɛːə sei].

40. The diphthongs in *bite* and *bout* are pronounced by the uneducated in many ways not permissible in standard English. The first element should be "clear" [a]. A "pure" [ɑ] would not be offensive here, though it is much less common;[47] but any pushing forward of the tongue beyond the [a] limit, any substitution of [æ] for [a], is not to be tolerated. The nasalising of these diphthongs adds to the unpleasant effect. Probably the best means of counteracting these tendencies is to insist on [ɑi] and [ɑu]; if the pure [ɑ] has been practised, as was suggested above, it will form a stepping-stone to the acquisition of good diphthongs.

Notice how a German pronounces these diphthongs; you will find that he dwells much longer on the first element than we do, and that it is more open.

The ending *-ile* in *agile, docile, fertile, futile, hostile, puerile* is pronounced [ail], and not [il] as used to be the case.

41. The next sounds in the series, obtained by raising the tongue a little higher than for [ɛ], are "middle" [e] and "close" [ẹ]. The vowel in *pen, get, fell* is usually the middle [e]; some speakers (perhaps mostly ladies) use the close [ẹ] here, but the very close [e], heard in French *été*, is not found in standard English. For ordinary purposes the sign [e] may serve to designate both [e] and [ẹ], as they are so closely connected. When unstressed, the [e] gives place to [ə]; thus unstressed *them* is [ðəm]. Notice that *'em* really goes back to the old form *hem*.

For [e] see the diagram on p. 122.

Observe the colloquial tendency to pronounce *get* as [git].

A fairly close [e] is in standard English the first element of the diphthong in *laid, tame, late,* etc. There is not one uniform vowel sound in these words; pronounce *aid* quite slowly, and you will notice that the tongue rises before the consonant is reached. The diphthong is long when a voiced sound follows it, short before a voiceless sound. Thus *laid* [leid] is longer than *late* [leit]. Test this statement by finding other words containing the diphthong, and pronouncing them to yourself or getting others to pronounce them. What is the quantity of the [ei] when the diphthong is final?

In vulgar speech the first element of the diphthong tends to [ɑ], sometimes almost to [ɔ].

Listen to a foreigner's pronunciation of English words containing this diphthong; what do you notice?

The vowel in *says* and *said* is short [sez, sed], as also in *ate* [et]. The pronunciation of *-ain* as [ein] in such words as *fountain, captain, bargain,* is a pedantic affectation.

How do you pronounce *villain, curtain*?

42. Two front vowels remain to be considered, the *i* sounds. Say *bid* and *bead*. You recognise that one is longer than the other; are they otherwise the same? Say *bid* and repeat it with the same vowel drawn out; then say *bead*, and repeat it with the vowel shortened. If you are careful in each case to change only the length, and not the quality of the vowel, you will perceive that the vowels in *bid* and in *bead* are different.

The vowel in *bid* is laxly articulated and is known as the open [ɪ]. In unstressed syllables (see § 38) it is often very open indeed, and when it is final, as in *very*, the tongue is raised very little higher than for close or even middle *e*. The sign for this sound is [e⸳] or [ɪ⸳]. (Here ⸳ means more close, ⸳ more open.) Can you hear any difference between the two vowels of *lily*?

The great phonetician Ellis remarked that the pronunciation of the *i* in *six* is the touchstone of foreigners, especially of those belonging to the Romance nations; they usually articulate it too tensely. Ask a Frenchman to say *fini*, and compare his sounds with those in *finny*.

Notice the frequent cockney pronunciation of *-y* as [ei], *e.g.*, in windy [wind*ei*].

Often [ə] is substituted for this sound, as in *unity, ability*, pronounced [juwnəti, ə´biləti], also in *April, visible*; but this is avoided by some speakers.

The [i] in the diphthongs [ai] and [ɔi], as in *buy, boy*, is very low.

In *bead* we have not a single vowel, but a kind of diphthong. If you utter it slowly, you will find that the tongue does not remain in a uniform position, but rises a little towards the end, the sound becoming closer. It may begin close, in which case the further rising reduces the passage so much that we have [j]; *bead* in this case is [bijd]. Or the vowel may begin fairly open and rise to the close position; then *bead* is [bɪid].[48] When the diphthong is followed by a voiceless sound, it is shortened; *beat* [bijt] [bɪit] is shorter than *bead*. Compare also *seed, seat, sit*; *feed, feet, fit*. Careful speakers pronounce *been* like *bean*, not like *bin*; most speakers, however, use the shortened form in ordinary speech.

For [i] see the diagram on p. 122.

In *dear, fear*, etc., we have a rather open vowel, of varying length, followed by [ɔ]; we may write [diə], but strictly it is [dɪə, dI·ə] and sometimes [dI:ə]. Before [r], as in *dearest*, the [ə] becomes faint or disappears. Standard English contains no [i] as close as the French [i] and the German [i:]. Convince yourself of this by asking foreigners to pronounce words containing these sounds, in their own language or in English.

Notice the frequent pronunciation of *ear, year*, as [jə:], and that of *dear* as [djə:].

We are now able to give the whole series of vowels from [i] to [ɑ] occurring in standard English.

close i (diagram, p. 122)
  \
  open ɪ
    \
    close e (diagram, p. 122)
      \
      middle *e*
        \
        open ɛ (diagram, p. 123)
          \
      more open æ
        \
        clear a (diagram, p. 123)
          \
            ɑ (diagram, p. 125)

It will be good practice for you to utter this series of sounds, from [ɑ] to [i] and *vice versa*, and long as well as short.

The raising of the tongue for the [i] sounds is best seen if the upper and lower teeth are kept well apart.

43. The back vowels.—When the front vowels have been carefully differentiated, the back vowels will be found to present little difficulty. Owing to the fact that the back of the tongue does not admit of so much variety of movement as the front of the tongue, the number of sounds in the series [ɑ] to [u] is smaller than in the series [a] to [i].

You will see that there is some resemblance between the sounds of the two series. Thus we had a lax [æ] and a tense [ɛ:] in the front vowels; and there are corresponding open *o* sounds when the tongue is raised a little at the back.

The articulation of these sounds is often unsatisfactory owing to the lower jaw not being moved down sufficiently, the teeth being hardly separated. The back vowels gain in quality (cp. § 36) if they are produced with lip rounding. The opening is large in the case of the sounds in which the tongue is only slightly raised; as it rises higher, the opening of the lips grows smaller, until for [u] it is only the size of the end of an ordinary lead pencil. This lip rounding is rare with southern English speakers who have not had special voice training; they usually bring together or separate the lips without rounding.

The short vowel sound in *not*, *what*, etc., is a laxly articulated, open [ɔ], much more open than any *o* in French or German, with the front of the tongue even lower than for [ɑ]. It is lengthened a little before a voiced final consonant, as in *dog* [dɔg]; but it should never be made quite long. The pronunciation [gɔ:d] for *God* is detestable. Before *ss* [s], *st* [st], *sp* [sp], *th* [θ], and *f, ff,* or *ph* [f], the long sound is occasionally heard. Determine whether in the following words you use the long or the short sound: *loss, ost, froth, cross, cough, soft, coffee, off, officer, cloth, moss, gospel*. Extend the inquiry to your friends.

When the short [ɔ] is in an unstressed syllable it either disappears entirely (as in *lesson*, where the [n] is syllabic, see § 24), or it may become [ə], as in *minor* [mainə], or it may become the sound [ö], which will be explained in

§ 44. Thus *October* is [ɔk´toubə] or [ök´toubə]; *connect* is [kɔ´nekt] only in precise speech, but usually [kö´nekt] or [kə´nekt].

The long [ɔ] in *law, laud, lord* is rather tensely articulated, certainly not so laxly as the short [ɔ].[49] Before voiceless sounds the vowel is somewhat shortened, as in *short* (compare *shawl* and *shot*). It is in standard English the only sound of stressed *or* (or *oar*) before a consonant;[50] there is no difference in sound between *laud* and *lord, fought* and *fort, stalk* and *stork, cawed* and *cord*. It is true that some speakers try to make a distinction. The long [ɔː] is not a simple long vowel, but really a diphthong of which the second element is [ə][51]; and in words containing a written *r*, these precise speakers somewhat lengthen the [ə] element. Thus they will say [lɔːᵊd] for *laud*, and [lɔːəd] for *lord*. It may be added that they generally do so only if the distinction has been spoken about, and they have expressed their firm belief in its existence; then, for a while, the [ɔːə] may be heard. A simple test, which the student should apply to his friends, is that of asking them to write down the word he utters. If he says [fɔːt], meaning *fought*, most people will write down *fort*, because the sound gives them no guidance, and the substantive is likely to occur to them first. Similarly, if he says [lɔːd], meaning *laud*, they will write down *lord*.[52]

The word *lore*, which hardly occurs in ordinary speech, is often pronounced [lɔːə] in order to distinguish it from *law*, the [ə] sound being much more distinct than in *law, more, bore*, etc. Consider the value of *-ore-* in *more water*, and in *more ink*.

There is much variation in the pronunciation of the words *daunt, flaunt, gaunt, gauntlet, haunch, haunt, jaundice, jaunt, launch, laundry, paunch, saunter, staunch, taunt, vaunt*. The general tendency seems to be in favour of [ɔː], not [ɑː].

When unstressed, the sound is often shortened to [ɔ] or [ö][53]; thus *autumnal* becomes [ɔ´tʌmnəl] or [ö´tʌmnəl]; *or* when stressed is [ɔ:], unstressed [ɔ] or [ö] or [ə].

A variety of the open [ɔ], not equally open in all speakers of standard English, is the first element in the diphthong found in *boy* [bɔi]. The pronunciation [böi[53]] is also heard.

In vulgar speech [ɔi] sometimes becomes [ɑi]; thus *boil* is pronounced [bɑil]. Only in *choir* (also written *quire*) is this pronunciation current in good speech.

44. Utter the sound usually called "long *o*" and found in *bode, boat*, etc,; you will observe that the sound is not uniform, as the tongue rises a little before the consonant is reached.[54] Indeed the action of the tongue is quite similar to what we noticed in the case of [ei] in § 41; and also to [i:j] or [I:i] in § 42, where, however, it is less obvious to the ear. The diphthongal character of the "long *o*" is so essential, that when a stranger merely says [o:no:] for *oh no!* we at once recognise that he is not English.

The first element of this diphthong is a middle [o], sometimes a fairly close [o]; in standard English the [o] is never so close as in French [o] or in German [ɔ:].[55] (Watch foreigners when they utter these sounds; notice how tensely they articulate, and how much more they round their lips than we do.) In cockney speech the first element is pronounced with the tongue lower and raised in front.—The second is a *u* sound; place a finger against the interval between the upper and lower teeth, and notice how they are brought a little closer towards the end of the diphthong. Observe also the action of the lips. The diphthong is longer before voiced than before voiceless continuants; verify this statement by saying, or getting others to say, *bode* and *boat, goad* and *goat, robe* and *rope, brogue* and *broke*.

In syllables that are weakly stressed, the first part of the diphthong becomes [o], [ö][56] or even [ə], the second part disappearing altogether. Thus *fellow* is in precise speech [felo:u], but in ordinary speech [felo, felö], and in careless (but not necessarily vulgar) speech [felə].[57] In "ladies' speech" the [öü] occurs even in stressed syllables, and may then be confidently described as a sign of affectation.

The prefix *pro-*, when stressed, is generally pronounced [prou]. In *process* and *progress* [prɔ] is sometimes heard; in the substantives *project* and *produce* it is the rule.

45. The *u* sounds are clearly parallel to the *i* sounds. In both cases we have a laxly articulated short sound, and a diphthong in which the tongue rises towards the end.

The short sound in *would, book,* etc., is open, and the sign for it is [ʊ]. Do you notice any difference in the length of the vowel sound in the words *should* and *put, pull* and *cook*? Observe others, if you are uncertain in your own case. (You will sometimes find it hard to determine what is your natural, instinctive way of pronouncing a word, when once you have grown accustomed to watching your own speech.)

When this [ʊ] is unstressed it becomes [ü][58] or [ə], or is dropped altogether. Thus *helpful* becomes [helpfül, helpfəl], and *should* becomes [ʃüd, ʃəd, ʃd, ʃt].

The vowel sound in *who* is not uniform. (See what was said about the corresponding *i* sound in § 42). It may begin as close [u][59], in which case the further rising towards the end reduces the passage so much that we have [w]; *who* in this case is [hu:w]. Or the vowel may begin fairly open and rise to the close position; then *who* is [hU:u]. When the diphthong is followed by a voiceless sound, it is somewhat shortened; *hoot* is [huwt] or [huut]; compare *root* with *rude*. A half-long vowel is now generally heard in *room*; some speakers make it quite short.

In unstressed syllables the first element is shortened and often becomes [ü]; thus *July* is [dʒüw´lai].

Before [ə] the diphthong loses its second element; *cruel* is [kruəl]. When the [ə] represents a written *r*, the first element often changes to a vowel with lower tongue position. Thus *poor* is pronounced [puə, poə], and some educated speakers of southern English even say [pɔː], riming with *door, floor*; but this can hardly be considered standard English. Notice also the various pronunciations of *your, sure*. Before spoken [r], as in *poorest, enduring*, the [ə] becomes very faint or disappears.

The so-called "long u" in such words as *due, dew, dude* consists of three parts. The second and third are the vowel sounds in *do*, which have just been discussed; the first is [j], which after voiceless sounds tends to become the voiceless [ç] and even [ʃ], as was mentioned in § 34. Thus *tune* is in ordinary speech [tjuwn], and often [tçuwn]; in careless speech it may even become [tʃuwn].

The *-ture* in *nature, creature, forfeiture*, etc., is generally pronounced [tʃə] [60]; the pronunciation [tjə] or [tjü] sounds affected in ordinary speech. *Venture* is usually [ventʃə], sometimes [venʃə], [ventjə], or [ventjü]. *Censure* is always [senʃə].

In *allude, *allusion, lute, lucent, luminous, *flute, salute,*absolute, *absolution, dissolute, *dissolution, *superstition, *Susan* both [uw] and [juw] may be heard; [uw] is probably more common in the words marked with an asterisk. Precise speakers prefer [juw] in all the words given. In *assume, presume* [juw] is regularly heard. As a rule [j] is not inserted after [r], [ʃ], [ʒ], or consonant plus [l].

Notice the pronunciation of *casual* [kæʒuəl] or [kæʒwəl], *sensual* [senʃuəl], *usual* [juwʒuəl] or [juwʒəl], *visual* [vizjuəl]. *Educate* is [edjukeit] or [edʒukeit]; careful speakers prefer the former.

As the "long *u*" begins with a consonantal sound it is correct to say *a uniform, a university, a union, a European, a eulogy*. To write *an* before such words is a gross mistake.

We find the [u] element changed in unstressed syllables; thus *value* becomes [væljü], *regular* becomes [regjülə, regjələ], and, very colloquially, [reglə].

We are now able to give the whole series of vowels from [u] to [ɑ] occurring in standard English:

      ü close u (diagram, p. 124)
        /
     open ʊ
     /
   close o (diagram, p. 124)
    /
ö middle *o*
 /
  open ɔ (diagram, p. 125)
 /
dark ɑ

Practise this series, as was suggested in § 42, in connection with the [i] to [ɑ] series.

FOOTNOTES:

[14] For the sake of convenience the nasal sounds, in producing which the breath does not also pass out through the mouth, *i.e.* which are not nasal vowels (see § 8), are included under "stops."

[15] Sounds in phonetic transcript are enclosed in square brackets.

[16] Also called labial.

[17] Also called dental.

[18] Also called palatal.

[19] Also called velar (from velum, for which see § 8) and more usually, but less accurately, guttural.

[20] An oral stop followed by [h] is called an aspirate. Aspirates are common in German, but practically unknown in standard French.

[21] Examples in the conventional spelling are printed in *italics*.

[22] *i.e.* at the end of a word, before a pause.

[23] When the aspiration is strongly marked, it forms a characteristic of the speech of the lower middle class in London and some home counties.

[24] The point stops are also called teeth or dental stops.

[25] On the other hand, in Somerset *clean, clod* are sometimes pronounced with [tl-].

[26] See footnote 8 on page 29.

[27] See footnote 8 on page 29.

[28] In standard English; in certain dialects the ending-*ing* is always pronounced [iŋg].

[29] The educated commonly say [buloun]; [bulɔin] is also heard.

[30] The hushing and hissing sounds are also called sibilants.

[31] See also § 45.

[32] Some speakers say [ə´souʃieit] but [ə´sousieiʃən], [i´nʌnʃieit] but [i´nʌnsieiʃən].

[33] In a great many cases lisping is due to an over-long tongue; or the tongue may be "tied," in which case the ligature is easily cut.

[34] The back of the tongue may also be raised to some extent; how does this explain the substitution of [w] for [r] which is sometimes heard?

[35] The rule may also be stated thus: *r* is only heard when a vowel follows in the same or the next word. "Vowel" must here be taken to include [j].

[36] The term "dark" here implies a deep and obscure resonance, with little friction.

[37] Contrast the [l] of *will* and *willing* (where its position between front vowels leads to forward formation).

[38] Some pronounce this word [sælv].

[39] Some pronounce this word [fɔlkən].

[40] These are modifications of the Scotch form of the word.

[41] [h] is described as voiceless; but it may also be produced with voice. We have seen that the vocal chords consist of a fleshy and a cartilaginous part: it is possible to let the former vibrate, while the latter is left open, and the breath passing through produces [h]. Try to utter this sound.

[42] The "neutral" vowel [ə], for which see § 38, requires less effort.

[43] Notice the faulty tendency to raise the tongue too high in uttering the first part of this diphthong; see § 40.

[44] However, there is a pronunciation of *are*, intermediate between the emphatic [ɑ:] and the unstressed [ə], which may be described as short [ɑ]. The *a* in the unstressed prefix *trans-*, and the second *a* of *advantageous* also have the sound of [ɑ] sometimes.

[45] Especially when it is final.

[46] Many cultivated people pronounce *girl* as [gɛəl]; but [gə:l] is to be preferred. *Clerk, sergeant* have [ɑ:], not [ə:]; also *Derby, Berkshire, Hertfordshire*.

[47] It is heard on the stage and in public speaking generally; in ordinary conversation it suggests the speech of a foreigner, especially if the [ɑ] element of the diphthong is lengthened.

[48] The first part is still more open in a common vulgar pronunciation of *tea, please*.

[49] For [ɔ:] see the diagram on p. 125.

[50] Exceptions are *borrow*, etc., *work, attorney*, etc.

[51] To pronounce this [ə] distinctly in such words as *law, saw* is a mistake.

[52] It is absurd to speak of *fort* and *caught, morn* and *dawn* as "cockney" rimes; they are perfectly good rimes in standard English; and a southern Englishman only shows ignorance by speaking of them as bad. Considering, however, that standard English is by no means universal, the would-be poet is advised to avoid these rimes.

[53] For [ö] see the note on p. 68.

[54] In the case of this diphthong as well as in that in *name, pail*, etc. (see § 41), untrained singers usually betray themselves by passing too soon to the second part of the diphthong.

[55] For [o] see the diagram on p. 124.

[56] [ö] is [o] pronounced with the whole body of the tongue more forward than usual. To the ear it gives an effect like that of French *eu* or German *ö*; but for these sounds the lips are rounded.

[57] The pronunciations [wində, pilə] for *window, pillow* are, however, avoided by educated speakers.

[58] [ü] is [u] pronounced with the whole body of the tongue more forward than usual. To the ear it gives an effect like that of French *u* or German *ü*; but for these sounds the lips are rounded.

[59] For [u] see the diagram on p. 124.

[60] See also § 29.

THE SOUNDS IN CONNECTED SPEECH

46. Let us take a familiar nursery rime as an example of simple conversational English; it will serve to give us some idea of the problems which have to be considered when we deal with the sounds of connected speech. This is the rime:

siŋ ə sɔŋ əv sikspəns | ə pɔkit ful əv rai | fɔːr ən tʍenti blækbəːdzz̬ | beikt in ə pai | wen ðə pai wəz oŭpnd | ðə bəːdzz̬ biˊgæn tə siŋ | wɔzn̩(t) ðæt ə deinti diʃ | tə set biˊfɔː ðə kiŋ.

47. Pedantically precise speech is as much out of place in the nursery as vulgar speech; therefore we do not say, siŋ eĭ sɔŋ ɔv sikspens.

Notice that the following words have **strong and weak forms**, a weak form being regularly used when they are not stressed:—

	weak	*strong*
a, an	ə, ən	ei, æn
the	ðə (before consonants) ði (before vowels)	ðij
has	həz,[61] əz, z	hæz
have	həv,[61] əv, v	hæv
had	həd,[61] əd, d	hæd
is	iz, z, s	iˑz
are	ɑ(r), ə(r)	ɑːə, ɑːr
was	wəz	wɔz
were	wə(r)	wəː(r), wɛːə(r)
can	kən, kn̩	kæn
shall	ʃəl, əl, l	ʃæl
will	əl, l	wil
could	kəd	kud
should	ʃəd, ʃd, ʃt, d	ʃud
would	wəd, əd, d	wud
he	hi,[62] i	hij
she	ʃi	ʃij
her	hə(r),[62] ə(r)	həː(r)

him	ɪm	him
his	ɪz	hiz
we	wi	wij
us	əs	ʌs
you	ju, jə	juw
them	ðəm, (əm)	ðem
your	jü(r), jɔ(r), jə(r)	juːə(r)
of	əv	ɔv
from	frəm, frm̩	frɔm
to	tə (before consonants)	tu
and	ənd, n̩d, ɔn, n̩	ænd
or	ɔ(r), ə(r)	ɔː(r)

The use of strong forms for weak ones in ordinary conversation is undoubtedly a fault, and should be avoided; much of the unnatural reading aloud in our schools is due to this cause. Foreigners who have lived long in England often fail in this respect when they have overcome almost all other difficulties. It is also not uncommon in the speech of colonials.

Notice [pens], but [sikspəns].

A word which forms the second part of a compound often changes in pronunciation, a weaker form being substituted. Compare *penny* and *halfpenny*, *board* and *cupboard*, *come* and *welcome*, *day* and *yesterday*, *ways* and *always*, *fast* and *breakfast*, *mouth* and *Portsmouth*, *land* and *England*, *ford* and *Oxford*.

The first letter of the second part is sometimes dropped; thus the *w* in *housewife* (case for needles, etc.) [hʌzif], *Greenwich, Harwich, Woolwich, Norwich, Keswick, Warwick* is no longer pronounced, nor the *h* in *shepherd, forehead, Clapham, Sydenham*, and in many words beginning with *ex-*, e.g., *exhale*,[63] *exhaust, exhibit, exhilarate, exhort*. The dropping of *h* in *neighbourhood* is vulgar.

Sometimes there is a change in the first part of a compound word. Compare *half* and *halfpenny*, *three* and *threepence*, *fore* and *forehead*, *break* and *breakfast*.

The stress of compounds like *sixpence* is discussed below ("blackbirds").

48. In *pocket* the second vowel is not middle [e], but a very laxly articulated variety of [ɪ], with the tongue only a little higher than for close [e]; see § 38. In the speech of elocutionists the middle [e] often appears here. They tell of the [gaːəden ɔv ijden], just as they succeed in pronouncing [devɪl] instead of [devəl], thus avoiding all offence; for [devəl] is said by common people, but [devɪl] only by the polite.

Notice that in *four-and-twenty* the *r* is pronounced, as it comes between vowels; but it is mute in *before the King*, where it comes before a consonant, as in the word *forth*. See § 32.

49. In *and* the *d* is dropped. Here it might be a case of assimilation; that is to say the *t* which immediately follows, and which is closely akin to it, might have changed it to [t], and the two would have fallen together.

In *sit down*, do you utter both [t] and [d]? If you speak naturally, you probably say [sidaun] or [sitaun]. What is your pronunciation of *hold tight, less zeal*?

In *cupboard* none but the absurdly precise pronounce the [p].

Assimilation of consonants is common in English, and the more colloquial the speech is, the more assimilation you are likely to find. Assimilation reduces the number of movements which have to be made, and thus represents a saving of trouble; and in colloquial speech we incline to take as little trouble as possible.

The general rule is, that when two sounds come together, those movements of articulation which are common to both are executed once only. Thus in *don't*,[64] the stopping of the passage for [n] also does duty for [t]; it is the opening of the passage which constitutes the [t]. In *stamp* the closure for [m] also does duty for [p]. In *witness* the closure for [t] remains for [n], which merely requires the opening of the nose-passage and vibration of the vocal chords.

Utter the word *clean*, and observe whether you produce the [k] in the same way as in *keen*; probably you will find that for the [k] of *clean* you open the closure only at the sides, leaving the centre of the tongue in contact, ready for the production of [l]. See whether anything similar happens when you say the word *atlas*.

Sometimes a voiced sound makes a neighbouring sound voiced, or a voiceless sound makes a neighbouring sound voiceless. Examples in the nursery rime are [bə:dzz̩] and [beikt]; find similar examples of the *s* of the plural[65] and the *ed* of the past participle, and determine in each case whether the final sound is voiced or voiceless. Try to find pairs like *lagged* and *lacked*, *bids* and *bits*.

Utter the words *apt*, *act*, and notice carefully when you make the closure for [t]; probably it is earlier than you would have thought. Do you make the [n] closure in *open* before or after the [p] opening?

In compound words, and in neighbouring words which belong closely together, assimilation is common. When one word ends in a voiceless sound and the other begins with a voiced sound, or *vice versa*, it is usually the second which prevails. Observe *cupboard* [kʌbəd], *raspberry* [rɑ:zbəri], *blackguard* [blægɑ:d], *bedtime* [betaim], *hold tight* [houltait].

Consider the pronunciation of *observe, obstacle, gooseberry, absolve, absolute*.

In careless speech [hɔ:ʃu] is heard for [hɔ:sʃu], [lædbru grouv] does duty for *Ladbroke Grove*, and [həsijn] for *has seen*. *Is she* is regularly pronounced [iʒ ʃi], or [iʃi] in quick conversation.

The nasals frequently change to suit the place of articulation of the *following* sound, as in *congress* [kɔŋres], *congregation* [kɔŋri´geiʃən], *anchor, concave, conclusion, concourse, concrete, syncope, tranquil, unctuous, pincushion* [piŋkuʃən], *infamous* [imfəməs], *Holland Park* [hɔləmpɑ:k]; or of the *preceding* sound, as in *second single* [sekŋsiŋgəl], *captain* [kæpm̩], *open the door* [oupm̩ ðə dɔ:], *cup and saucer* [kʌpm̩sɔ:sə]. The examples from *pincushion* onwards occur only in distinctly careless speech.

The change of [s] to [z] in *house, houses* [haus, hauziz], shows a different kind of assimilation.

50. The dropping of *d* in *four-and-twenty* might also be due to the desire to **simplify a group of consonants**; and this will seem the more likely explanation if we notice that the *d* of *and* is generally dropped before a consonant, but kept before a vowel. Compare *you and Ida, bread and butter*; if you drop the *d* in the first instance, or utter it in the second, you are equally wrong. Such simplifying is fairly common in educated speech; most people drop the *t* in *often*, and the *p* in *empty* (where it has no etymological justification), and *jumped*; in colloquial speech *don't know* is [dʌnou]. In quite careless speech you may notice consonants dropped in such words as *acts, insects*, but this is clearly a licence which cannot be permitted in the class-room. Indeed these groups of consonants should be articulated with great care. Nothing so quickly gives an effect of slovenly speech as the slurring of consonants, where it is not generally adopted.

In ordinary speech numerous instances occur of this tendency to simplify groups of consonants, *d* and *t* being the sounds most frequently dropped.

d is not pronounced in *handkerchief* [hæŋkətʃif], *handsome* [hænsəm], *Windsor* [winzə], *Guildford* [gilfə·d], *Ingoldsby* [iŋgəlzbi], *Wednesday* [wenzdi].[66]

The *d* in *friends, grandfather* is also often dropped; and, in very careless speech, the *d* of such words as *old, cold, child, thousand, kindness, landlord*.

t is not pronounced in *christen* [krisən], *glisten* [glisən], *hasten* [heisən], *listen* [lisən], *moisten* [mɔisən], *apostle* [ə´pɔsəl], *bustle* [bʌsəl], *castle* [kɑ:səl], *epistle* [i´pisəl], *gristle* [grisəl], *hustle* [hʌsəl], *ostler* [ɔslə], *pestle* [pesəl], *rustle* [rʌsəl], *thistle* [θisəl], *trestle* [tresəl], *whistle* [wisəl], *wrestle* [resəl], **Westbourne* [wesbən], **Westminster* [wesminstə], *Christmas* [krisməs], *chestnut* [tʃesnət], *coastguard* [kousgɑ:d], *often* [ɔ:fən], *soften* [sɔ:fən], *mortgage* [mɔ:gidʒ], **directly* [di´rekli], **exactly* [i´gzækli], *postpone* [pous´poun], *waistcoat* [weiskət, weskət], *bankruptcy* [bæŋkrəpsi].

In very careless speech the *t* of such words as *slept, swept, wept* is dropped; also in *acts, facts, insects, sects*.

Notice the French *rosbif, bifteck*.

th is not pronounced in *asthma* [æsmə], *isthmus* [isməs] and (carelessly) in *depths*.

p is not pronounced in *empty* [emti], *jumped* [dʒʌmt], *tempt* [temt], *attempt* [ə´temt], *contempt* [kən´temt], *peremptory* [pər´emtəri], *symptom* [simtəm],[67] *sapphire* [sæfaiə], *Sappho* [sæfou].

c is not pronounced in *corpuscle* [kɔ:´pʌsəl], *muscle* [mʌsəl], *victuals* [vitl̩z], *indict* [in´dait].[68]

So many educated speakers say [ɑ:st] for *asked*, that this pronunciation must be regarded as no longer incorrect.

What is the usual pronunciation of *next station*?

In careful speech the simplifications marked with an asterisk are avoided, as also such pronunciations as [ail dʒʌssij] for *I'll just see*, [difikl̩ kwestʃn̩z] for *difficult questions*. The omission of [k] in the pronunciation of *arctic* and *antarctic* and of [g] in *recognise* is generally regarded as faulty.

Unfamiliar groups of consonants at the beginning of words are simplified by dropping the first sound; notice the simplification of

    bd   in *bdellium*;
    chth in *chthonian*;
    gn   in *gnaw, gneiss, gnome, gnostic*;
    gz (x) in *Xerxes* [zəːksijz], *Xenophon*;
    kn   in *knee, knit, know*, etc.;
    mn   in *mnemonic*;
    phth in *phthisis* [θaisis], also [taisis];
    pn   in *pneumatic, pneumonia*;
    ps   in *psalm, pseudo-, Psyche, psychic* [saikik], *psychology*, etc.;
    pt   in *ptarmigan, Ptolemy*;
    sw   becomes *s* in *sword* (observe also *answer*);
    wr   in *wreck, write*, etc.

Similarly, an unfamiliar group at the end of a word is simplified, usually by dropping the last sound; notice—

ln in *kiln* (some do not drop this *n*);
mb in *bomb, catacomb, climb, comb, dumb, hecatomb, lamb, limb, plumber, succumb, tomb*;
mn in *autumn, column, condemn, contemn, hymn, limn, solemn*.

(The opposite tendency is found in vulgar speech, where [vɑːmint] is said for *vermin*, [draund] for *drown*.)

Observe *drachm* [dræm], *yacht* [jɔt], *impugn* [imˈpjuwn], *physiognomy* [fiziˈɔnəmi], *diaphragm* [daiəfræm], *paradigm* [pærədaim], *phlegm* [flem], *sign* [sain], *feign, reign, foreign, benign*.

51. In [rai] we have a diphthong. It is worth noting that the English diphthongs [ai, au, ɔi, ei, ou], etc., all have the **stress** on the former element.

Blackbirds and *black birds*: in the spelling we distinguish these by writing the first as one word, the second as two. What difference is there in the sounds? If you listen carefully, you will find that the second vowel in the compound word is just a little shorter than in *birds* standing alone, and that in *blackbirds* the opening of the closure for [k] is not heard, while in *black birds* it may be audible. The chief difference, however, lies in the **stress of the compound word**. *Blackbirds* is an example of descending stress [>], *black birds* is pronounced with level stress [=], perhaps with ascending stress [<].

Take the following compound words or groups, and classify them according to their stress:—

Sixpence, rainbow, good morning, looking glass, moonshine, bravo!, twenty-four, twenty-four men, High Street, London Road, waterspout, right of way, undo, Mr Jones, Park Lane, season ticket, sunflower, Hongkong, steel pen, Chinese, hallo! bill of fare, earthquake, sea wall, Bond Street, Grosvenor Square, fourteen, Hyde Park.

Try to deduce some rules from these examples. It has been said that level stress contrasts, and uneven stress unites the ideas expressed by the compound words; do you agree with this?

Notice what difficulty our level stress gives to the German; he will utter *steel pen, Hyde Park*, etc., with descending stress. Do so yourself, and observe how strange it sounds.

Notice the difference in stress of

Substantive or Adjective	**Verb**
absent	*to absent*
accent	*to accent*
consort	*to consort*
converse	*to converse*
desert	*to desert*

prefix	*to prefix*
present	*to present*
Substantive	**Verb**
proceeds	*to proceed*
produce	*to produce*
project	*to project*
protest	*to protest*
rebel	*to rebel*
record	*to record*
refuse	*to refuse*
Substantive	**Adjective**
compact	*compact*
instinct	*instinct*
minute	*minute*

Some words of two syllables have the stress on the first or the second syllable according to their place in the sentence. Consider the accent of the italicised words in the following sentences: They sat *outside*. An *outside* passenger. Among the *Chinese*. A *Chinese* lantern. His age is *fifteen*. I have *fifteen* shillings. Some fell by the *wayside*. A *wayside* inn. Try to find a rule governing these cases.

The stresses in a sentence are considered in § 54.

When would be pronounced as voiceless [ʍ] by some, hardly by a southern English nurse saying the rime (§ 46). Notice how the tongue moves forward as the [n] passes over into the [ð] in *when the*.

Was is in the weak form because it is quite unstressed; but notice: [wɛːə ju riːəli ðɛːə? jes, ai wɔz].

52. In *opened*, observe carefully how the consonants are articulated, and put their action down in writing.

How many syllables are there in *opened, bubbles, chasms, mittens*?

Probably you have no difficulty in understanding and answering this question, but if asked to describe **a syllable** you might hesitate, for it is not easy.

Utter [ɑ] and then [t]; which carries farther, which has greater fulness of sound or sonority? If you wished to attract the attention of some one, and were only allowed to utter one of these two sounds, you would prefer [ɑ] without hesitation. Why is [ɑ] more sonorous than [t]? Because, whereas [t] is only a brief noise, in [ɑ] the current of breath is rendered musical by the vibration of the vocal chords, and has a free passage through the wide open mouth. Indeed [ɑ] is the most sonorous of all sounds. It is clear that voiced sounds are more sonorous than voiceless, vowels than consonants, continuants than stops. The liquids and nasals stand between vowels and consonants in point of sonority; they are voiced and with either a fair passage through the mouth or a free passage through the nose. A good deal naturally depends on the force and the pitch of the sounds; a whispered [ɑ] may not carry so far as a forcible [s].

Now if a sound with good carrying power has for its neighbours sounds that do not carry far, it helps them to be heard; notice how such weakly sonorous sounds as [t] or [p] occurring in the words of a song are quite clearly heard at the other end of a large concert hall. They are carried along by the full sounding vowels, as the greater volume of air employed causes more pressure, and hence a more forcible and louder release. It is the sounds of greater sonority that carry the syllable, which term is also applied to a vowel standing alone, or beside other vowels of practically equal sonority. In English, the syllable is generally carried by vowels; sometimes also by liquids and nasals, which are then called **syllabic**.[69]

Rules for dividing words into syllables are given in most grammars, and are required for writing and printing; but they do not always represent the actual state of things. When a consonant comes between two vowels, it really belongs to both syllables. In *leaving* we pronounce neither *lea-ving* nor *leav-ing*.

From the phonetic point of view we may think of words and groups of words as consisting of a series of sounds of varying sonority. We may indicate the sonority very roughly by lines; if we connect their top ends, we shall obtain a curve. Thus the word *sonority* might be represented as follows (no attempt is here made at scientific accuracy).

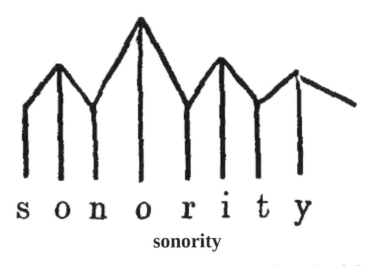

sonority

The curves will represent a series of waves; and each of these waves is a syllable.

Began: notice the quality of the vowel in the first, unstressed syllable of this word. It is higher than any real *e* sound, and is very laxly articulated. It occurs also in *before, enough, inquire*; find other words in which it occurs. Is it the same sound as the second vowel in *lily*?

To sing: read the sixth line quite naturally and see whether you say [tə] or [tu]; get friends to read it, and find out what they say.

When you wish to ascertain how a friend pronounces some particular sound, do not tell him what this sound is, or he may pronounce it not naturally, but in what he believes, or has been told, is "the correct pronunciation."

Try to ascertain the pronunciation of these sentences: *What are you going to do to-morrow morning? I'm going to answer letters.*

Wasn't that: *was* is here in the strong form (§ 47); are weak forms found at the beginning of a sentence? Notice the syllabic [n]; also the simplification of the group of consonants by the omission of [t]. What is the weak form of *that*? When is it used?

The remaining words present nothing of special interest.

53. We may now consider the **stress of the sentence**. For this purpose it is sufficient to consider the most sonorous part of each syllable, generally speaking a vowel. We may distinguish stress and absence of stress, which we can designate by the signs / and ×; extra strong stress will be //, and secondary stress \. The first line of Sing a Song of Sixpence, will then run: —

$$// \times / \times // \backslash$$

Here "sing" and "six" have the strongest stress; "song" has ordinary stress.

Secondary stress is given to that syllable of a word which is stressed, but has not the chief stress; thus the stresses in *energetic* may be written \ × / ×.

The nursery rhyme then shows the following stresses:—

```
      // × / × // \
    × // × / × //
      // × \ × // \
     // \ × //
    // × / × // \
   × // × / × //
  // × / × // × /
 × // × / × //
```

Perhaps you do not read the poem in this way; mark the stresses for yourself, without looking at the book.

Accept no statements without verifying them.

53A. It will have struck you that you have really been scanning the poem. Hitherto you may have done it by means of the signs ‒ and ˘, taken from Latin prosody, where they stand for "long" and "short." Consider the question which of these two systems of scansion is the more accurate and the more convenient.

53B. It may also strike you that in reading the poem we do not make a pause at the end of each word; and of course we do not read it "all in one breath." How many breaths do you require for reading it slowly? for reading it quickly? What guides you in finding places for your pauses? Take any dozen lines of prose and read them aloud; notice where you pause for breath. The words which are read together in one breath are called a *breath* *group*. After considering several passages from this point of view, you will realise that good reading depends to some extent on the choice of suitable places for taking breath. Let your friends read to you, and observe how they manage their breath.

54. We have spoken several times of stress, and you have probably followed without difficulty. What is stress? Utter the series of sounds [´atata], then [a ´tata], and [ata´ta].[70] You use more force for the stressed than for the unstressed vowels, that is to say, you put more breath into them. Place your hand close in front of your lips as you say the above sounds, and you will notice a distinct increase of breath as the stressed syllable is uttered.

We use this stress for purposes of emphasis; generally speaking, we expend more breath on those syllables of a word, or words of a sentence, which are more important for the meaning. We may say that English sentence stress is guided by logical considerations. Is this equally true of French? of German? Has anything struck you about the stress in French, or in English as spoken by a Frenchman?

55. Stress, due to force of breath, is not the only means of accentuation at our disposal. We can also produce various effects by changing the *pitch* of the voice. When the pitch of a voice hardly varies at all, we consider it monotonous. Certain clergymen have acquired the habit of reading the Church service in monotone; consider whether this has any advantage or disadvantage. When there is very great and regular or monotonous variation of pitch in a voice, we call it a "sing-song."

In standard speech there is moderate variation of pitch; it becomes considerable only in dramatic and oratorical declamation, when a skilled use of pitch variations may produce a deeply moving or highly stirring effect, somewhat resembling that produced by song.

Observe the pitch changes in ordinary speech. The most obvious case is the rise of pitch in questions, in contrast with the tendency to lower the pitch in a statement. Even though we have the same order of words as in a statement, this change of pitch alone suffices to show that a question is being asked. Say: *You are going out* and *You are going out?* Try to say *Are you going out?* with the same falling pitch as in *You are going out*, and observe the strange effect. Determine the changes of pitch in such questions as: *Is your brother tall or short? Is your uncle's house in the town or in the country?* Notice that joy or any great excitement leads to the use of a higher pitch than usual.

Sometimes the pitch may rise or fall, or rise and fall, or fall and rise during the utterance of a single vowel. Say *No* in a doubtful, a questioning, a decided, and a threatening tone, and observe the pitch. If you wish to represent it roughly, you may use \ for fall in pitch, / for a rise, ∧ for a rise and fall, ∨ for a fall and rise.

56. We have devoted our attention mainly to standard English as it is spoken in ordinary life, because it is important to train the ear so that it perceives the sounds and ceases to be misled by the conventional spelling. Only when we can hear what sounds our pupils actually utter, only when we have a fair idea of the way in which they produce these sounds, are we in a position to correct what is faulty in the mother tongue, or to impart the sounds of a foreign language with any prospect of success. Hints have been given as to some of the faulty tendencies likely to be found; the teacher whose ear has been trained in the manner here suggested will be able to add to their number without difficulty, and probably with growing interest. In this respect every county presents its own problems, and many still require to be recorded; every teacher can help by contributing his own observations.

No observer can fail to be struck by the different degrees of care with which most individuals speak English under different circumstances. In their talk among themselves, children, especially young boys, are often extremely careless; at home we find various degrees of care, much depending on the example set by the parents and the influence of governesses and nurses. In talking to educated strangers, we are usually careful in our pronunciation. If we occupy a position which makes it necessary to speak to large numbers, we must be particularly careful, and that in several respects: the voice must be pleasant, carry far, and have good staying power.

57. A pleasant voice is to a certain degree a natural gift; it depends on the quality of the vocal chords, the shape of the roof of the mouth, and so on. Many voices are spoilt by bad habits, such as excessive nasalising, or very high pitch. The teacher of elocution often gives valuable criticism and help here. Listen attentively to any criticisms which your friends make about your voice.

The voice of a public speaker (which includes the class teacher and college lecturer no less than the clergyman, actor, or politician) must carry far. His words must penetrate to every hearer, even in a large hall. If there is any straining to catch his words, those words will not produce their best effect. *The chief requirement is not loudness, but distinctness.* He must articulate more carefully than in ordinary conversation: unstressed vowels will have greater importance and be less reduced, consonants will never be slurred over. The stressed vowels are the most important of all because they are the most sonorous sounds and help the others (see § 52); he will let the vocal chords vibrate longer for them, to reinforce their value, and he will produce them in such a way that they give their characteristic sound most clearly. For this purpose he will find it best to articulate more tensely (this applies also to the consonants) than in ordinary speech; and a distinct rounding of the lips for the back vowels will enable him to add to their value. He will prefer to keep the tongue point well forward in the mouth for [l]. This and other hints he may obtain from the teacher of elocution.

However pleasant a voice may be, and however far it may carry, it will yet be of little use if it tires soon; it must have staying power. This again is to some extent a natural gift; the throat may be constitutionally weak. Training, however, can do very much to improve the powers of endurance. Above all, good breathing is essential; hints have been given in § 4 how this may be assured, and the teacher cannot be recommended too warmly to give from 15 to 25 minutes every morning to breathing exercises; he will be amply repaid for the time spent in that way by the greater ease with which he gets through his teaching, and by the inevitable improvement in his general health. It has also been pointed out above that bad ventilation and dust are calculated to interfere with his voice. Another suggestion may be helpful: to keep the tongue as forward in the mouth as possible. The average tongue position in many southern English teachers is too far back in the mouth, and this is found to lead to serious fatigue; it may indeed be regarded as one of the main causes of "teachers' sore throat."

It is in giving advice on the management of the voice for public speaking that trustworthy teachers of elocution are most helpful. When they make dogmatic statements as to how a sound or word is or should be pronounced, their guidance is not equally satisfactory, and the student is earnestly recommended always to test their statements himself. The same request is addressed to him with regard to the present book; if it arouses interest, there is no harm if it also arouses opposition.

FOOTNOTES:

[61] These forms are found, for instance, at the beginning of questions; thus *have you been there?* is [həv ju bijn ðɛə]. They are also found after vowels, e.g., *I had done so*, [ai həd dʌn sou].

[62] See the note on p. 72.

[63] When contrasted with *inhale*, this word is also pronounced [eksheil].

[64] The change in the quality of the vowel is interesting; possibly *don't* preserves the old pronunciation of the vowel in *do*.

[65] Strictly speaking the *s* of the plural was always voiced in the older language, and it is in *cats, tips* that we have assimilation.

[66] The first *d* is sometimes heard in the pronunciation of this word.

[67] It should, however, be noted that in passing from [m] to [t] there is a transitional sound or "glide" which has the value of a faint [p].

[68] The *c* in *victuals* and *indict* has no etymological justification, as may be seen from the middle English spelling (*vitaille, endite*).

[69] For syllabic *m* see § 22; for syllabic *n*, § 24; for syllabic *l*, § 33.

[70] The mark ´ *precedes* the stressed syllable.

APPENDIX I
Exercises.

1. How is *-ious* pronounced in *gracious, bilious, victorious*?

2. How is *-ion* pronounced in *motion, onion, criterion, vision*, and *Ionian*?

3. How is *-ial* pronounced in *labial, judicial, martial, partiality*?

4. What difference in pronunciation, if any, do you make between *hire* and *higher, lyre* and *liar, cure* and *(s)kewer, alms* and *arms*?

5. Consider the value of *oar* in *roar* and in *roaring*, and the value of *air* in *pair* and in *pairing*.

6. Determine the vowel sounds corresponding to the italicized letters in ch*i*ld, ch*i*ldren; wom*a*n, wom*e*n; r*ea*d (infinitive), r*ea*d (past participle); s*ay*, s*ay*s; dr*ea*m, dr*ea*med; l*ea*p, l*ea*ped; h*ea*r, h*ea*rd; c*a*n, c*a*n't; d*o*, d*o*n't; gentlem*a*n, gentlem*e*n.

7. Write in transcript the words italicized:

    a. I have *learned* much from this *learned* man.

    b. He has *aged* a good deal. He is *aged*.

    c. I *used* to *use* it; you *used* it too.

Try to account for the pronunciation of *used* in the sense of "was accustomed" (see § 49).

8. Transcribe your pronunciation of *halfpenny, twopence, threepence*. Show the difference between the English and the French pronunciation of *franc*, and between the English and the German pronunciation of *mark*.

9. A waiter was heard to remark pathetically that he never *could* tell whether a customer wanted "cold lamb" or "cold ham." What caused his uncertainty?

10. The pronunciation of the children of Walworth attending the Church schools has given much concern to Canon Horsley, who says that in their

speech "I've been to take her home" becomes "binter tiker rome," "Oh, shake hands" becomes "ow shy cans," and "I've been having a game" becomes "binnavinagime." Consider the pronunciation suggested by this rough transcription, transcribe it more carefully, and comment on such features of the Walworth dialect as it illustrates.

11. You are familiar with the term "alliteration," and know that it is a favourite device of cheap journalism. Criticise the alliteration in the following scare-lines: CITY CLERK CHASED. THIEF TAKEN. SOLICITOR SHOT.

12. Mention words in which the following letters are written but not sounded: *b, g, gh, k, l, m, n, t, w*.

13. Comment on the following statement: "The letters *l* and *r* are called trills, because there is a vibration in the sounds, or in some part of the vocal apparatus by which we pronounce them."

14. Consider this statement: "The *ai* in *fair*, *ea* in *lead*, *ie* in *field*, *ei* in *receive*, are none of them true diphthongs; they are more or less clumsy ways of showing the length of an elementary vowel-sound."

15. "English has two *e* sounds, as in *fed*, *feed*, and four *u* sounds, as in *but*, *pull*, *fur*, *fool*." Do you agree with this?

16. Why does *crystal* look nicer than *kristle*, which represents the same sounds? Account for such spellings as Edythe, Smythe, Whyte.

17. Say quickly but distinctly:

>   She sells sea-shells in a salt-fish shop.
>
>   Is Stephen Smith's son a smith too?
>
>   How many houses had Harry Hall?
>
>   Long and loudly little Lily laughed.
>
>   The skilled dentist extracted the three teeth.
>
>   Do you want the thick thread or the thin?
>
>   In silence he sat on the sands by the silvery sea.
>
>   A boat is floating over the ocean.

> With a loud shout he came out of the house.
>
> The first question Charles asked was strange.
>
> Three grey geese in the green grass grazing.

18. Discuss the old-fashioned form of address "mine host." Do you say "an historical novel"? "a (or an) hotel at Folkestone"? How do you pronounce "the Grand Hotel"? Transcribe your pronunciation of "I gave her her hat."

19. What is the derivation of *ventriloquist*? Does the term correctly indicate the way in which ventriloquists produce their sounds? Which sounds do you think most likely to give them difficulty?

20. In the French of the 12th century *l* under certain circumstances became a vowel; thus *altre* became *autre* and *chevals* became *chevaus*. How do you explain this change? Point to a similar change in English.

21. How would you teach a foreigner to pronounce the English *th* sounds?

22. Little children say *pease* for *please*, *gamma* or *granma* for *grandma*, *dess* for *dress*, *tocking* for *stocking*. Illustrate the tendency shown in these examples from the speech of grown-up people.

23. Comment on the little child's pronunciation of *tsain* for *chain*, *fee* for *three*, *noder* for *another*, and *bafyoom* for *bathroom*.

24. Consider carefully the question, why the pronunciation of a foreign language presents difficulties; draw on any foreign language you know for illustrations.

25. The Latin *camera* is our *chamber*, *numerus* our *number*, Latin *humilis* our *humble*, Latin *similare* our *(re)semble*. Account for the *b* in the English words.

26. Consider the value of *ure* in *sure, pure, nature, figure*.

27. What light is thrown on the pronunciation of the past by the following quotations:

> (*a*) While he, withdrawn, at their mad labour smiles,
>   And safe enjoys the Sabbath of his toils. (Dryden.)

> (*b*) Dreading even fools, by flatterers besieg'd,

And so obliging that he ne'er oblig'd. (Pope.)

(c) *Cóntemplate* is bad enough, but *bálcony* makes me sick. (Rogers.)

(d) The dame, of manner various, temper fickle,
Now all for pleasure, now the conventicle. (Colman.)

(e) There is little doubt that in the pronunciation of *successor* the antepenultimate accent will prevail. (Walker.)

(f) To ketch [catch] him at a vantage in his snares. (Spenser.)

(g) Yet he was kind, or, if severe in aught,
The love he bore to learning was in fault.
(Goldsmith.)

28. Determine which sounds are represented by *ea* in the following words: *bear, beard, bread, bead, yea, create, realm, leap, leapt, hearken*; and by *eo* in the following words: *yeoman, people, leopard, re-open*.

29. Determine which sounds are represented by *oi* in the following words: *boil, heroic, choir, tortoise, turquoise, coincide*; and by *ou* in the following words: *south, southern, mourn, journal, though, thought, uncouth*.

30. Determine which sounds are represented by *g* in the following words: *gem, goal, gaol, gill, gibberish, fatigue, gnaw*; and by *ough* in the following words: *trough, through, thorough, sough, cough, rough, plough, lough*.

31. A character in one of Miss Braddon's novels says: "Supernumery—it's no use, I don't think anybody ever did know how many syllables there are in that word." What is it that leads to the shortening of this word in uneducated speech? Mention similar cases of shortening.

CPSIA information can be obtained
at www.ICGtesting.com
Printed in the USA
BVHW021412110423
662129BV00010B/721